IMAGINING WELFARE

Anti-bureaucratic Social Work

Malcolm Payne

VENTURE PRESS

BASW website: http://www.basw.co.uk

Published by
VENTURE PRESS
16 Kent Street
Birmingham
B5 6RD

British Library Cataloguing-in-Publication Data
A catalogue record for this book is available from the British Library

ISBN: 1 86178 040 0   (paperback)

Cover design by:
Western Arts
194 Goswell Road
London
EC1V 7DT

Printed in Great Britain

CONTENTS

LIST OF FIGURES

FOREWORD AND ACKNOWLEDGEMENTS

I have always been a committed believer in the value of high-quality social work practice, and yet I have also always been interested in management. People have sometimes told me that these dual interests are peculiar: management is, in some views, inconsistent with high-quality social work. From time to time my writings have been criticised as naive because I have assumed that there is some possibility of and worth in getting management to support good social work. Yet equally, many social workers complain about the quality of the management that they are subjected to, and the ill-effects of bureaucracy on the lives of their clients. Indeed, we are all prone to complain about its ill-effects on all our lives.

Years ago, Tony Hall and I used to teach management together on a social work course, and he would start by writing 'management' on the chalkboard and asking people to call out their responses. The outcome was always a board full of hostility about the damage management does to social work practice, and not one good word. We used to regard our course as a process of persuading students to look at the possibility that managing their work was a valid and useful process. Perhaps we did this with success, because some of those students are now senior managers in social services departments. Two or three weeks ago, having stolen this teaching idea from him and used it ever since, I got a two-pronged response from students. The hostility and anger was still there, but so also was a demand that the management of social work should be better: gender was now a big issue, too.

This book is about social work practice which is concerned with management. Concerned in two different ways: with the role of social work practice as a way of overcoming bad management's effects on the lives of our clients and with social work practice valuing and developing good management in its own organisations.

Why is this book appearing in a series which looks forward to social work in a new millennium? My answer to this is that we have understood in the 20th century that social work is not the sort of profession in which workers have 'individual practitioner responsibility' for their work. It is integral to social work that it is done in organisations, and that a lot of work is not done with clients, patients or service users (whatever in different settings and fashions we call the people we work with) but on their behalf in other organisations. This kind of work is typical of social work: indeed it partly defines social work. I say this because other professions do not see it as their role, and social workers in many settings have turned out to be very good at contributing this kind of work to multiprofessional work. However, the crucial contribution of social work is not in itself management; it is making sure that the management of other organisations meets the needs of our clients, and as a direct corollary it means making sure social work organisations meet those needs effectively too.

So in the 21st century, we have to see social work as crucially concerned with organisations. We also have to strengthen our existing skills in understanding and making the best use of organisations for our clients. In this book, I am making the argument for seeing social work in this way and I am also trying to pick out from social work ideas what we can do in this area of practice.

Conversations with Margaret Reith about her work led to the title and approach of this book. I greatly value her ideas and professional skill which contribute to my writing here, as elsewhere. Much of what I have learned about advocacy and which appears in Chapter 3, I have learned from working with Jane Dalrymple, and I thank her for what I have gained. Gurid Aga Askeland read an early draft and made useful comments based on her extensive experience of being a social work manager and teaching about it. Only I am responsible for what is said and unsaid, however.

Malcolm Payne
Penarth

Chapter 1
BUREAUCRACY AND ACCOUNTABILITY

Alex Macmillan's wedding

Mr Macmillan was dying of cancer in his front room. He had been in hospital, had all the treatments and, some months later, had been discharged to die. It would be a few weeks at most; the family all knew. Because of the illness, he had been forced to give up work almost eighteen months before. On discharge, his wife had given up work to care for him. So money was tight. So Jane, his social worker, had been after the cancer charities to pull in a bit extra on top of the social security, to see the family through. And with success: a grant was being made to cover the costs of extra travel during the hospital period, heating and equipment for the home and a variety of other things. The family had laid out the money from their savings; now some of it was coming back in to help with the final few weeks.

Mr Macmillan's son, Alex, had been planning to get married next year, and when the inevitable end became obvious, he brought the marriage forward. However, Mr Macmillan could no longer get to the church. So, plans were changed and the reception would be around Mr Macmillan's bed in the front room. There would be flowers, a buffet, celebrations. Mr Macmillan would be the centre of them all, as he had been to the family for these past twenty-odd years.

There was just the problem of the cost. As Mrs Macmillan said to Jane: was there any chance of the grant coming through in time to help with the wedding? Jane checked: and no, the charity was processing the grant; it would be made but not until a week or so after the reception.

Jane could see no alternative but to pay the grant from her own money now, and when the money came through, ask the Macmillan's to let her have it back. Still, to do so would be against all the rules, and if it were found out, she would lose her job. So it would be a handshake agreement, rather than an arrangement to be written down. This is because it would be a misuse of the grant to pay it to herself. It would be contrary to the financial regulations that local government officers must abide by, to stop them fiddling public or charitable money. The most she could lose was the two hundred pounds. She asked if the Macmillan's minister of religion would note her intentions. He was glad to do so.

Mrs Macmillan was delighted; the reception was a great success; Mr Macmillan died a few days later. When the grant came, Mrs Macmillan paid the two hundred pounds straight over to Jane. Her's is a family which, like many others across the country, will always know and value what social workers can do.

1

But why was it necessary? Isn't it all just bureaucracy? Well, no; you can understand the reasons for the rules. It would be possible for a social worker to receive money and not pay it over to a client, claiming that she was owed money from some previous arrangement. There are examples in the past of workers managing to steal money owing to members of the public.

But why should the social worker have to do this? Isn't it obvious that the rules should have been relaxed? Any official in any sort of organisation, if they have a reasonable amount of experience, will have gone through something like this. I certainly have. Fortunately, I have usually had a boss who has been quite reasonable. I would have gone to my boss, explained what I was going to do and asked him to make a note. Then, if it came out for some reason, someone else would know the circumstances and it would be in writing in advance. I might get rapped over the knuckles, but we would probably not be in sacking territory. I can hear him: 'Fine, Malcolm, fine. You go ahead; I'll cover for you'. However, I would not have trusted some bosses, just as Jane could not trust her boss. Jane was astute to find someone above reproach to do the same for her if it went wrong.

I would not advocate this sort of thing, but it happens. It is social workers getting round rules which do not fit the particular situation. It is anti-bureaucratic social work.

Inflexibility is bad management
Having to get round the rules in this way should not be necessary. At best, it is bad management because the rules do not achieve the ultimate purpose of their existence. It is bad management in at least two different ways. First, the cancer charity should have had a procedure for speeding up a payment because their purpose is in reducing the distress of illness. If the payment comes too late, they cannot meet this ultimate purpose. It really is necessary to be prepared to be quick when routinely dealing with people who are in serious trouble.

The second way in which it was bad management was that the social services department (SSD) should have had an open process for self-authorisation. It should not rely on the social worker having the self-confidence (and the money) to step out of line or a boss being reasonable. Sensible discretion which people feel they can use should be built into any system. Not allowing the use of discretion leads to the risk of people working tricks to do the things they need to do, and the tricks leading to misuse of money and poor accounting.

Inflexibility in organisations has consequences for service users and members of the public and is often called 'bureaucracy'. Inflexible behaviour in workers is called 'bureaucratic behaviour'. Bureaucracy and bureaucratic behaviour are inflexibility in doing the work of an organisation and arises from excessive compliance with procedures and regulations so that the organisation's purposes are not achieved efficiently.

Reasons for bureaucratic inflexibility

Of course, there are reasons for bureaucratic inflexibility and, again, anyone with a modicum of experience in local government or in any large organisation will know what they are. The inflexibility is a protection for officers and councillors against pressure for misuse of power. It allows them to show that they have complied with regulations and procedures. Jane wanted to help the Macmillan's. Yet occasional clients make aggressive demands for more than they should have. Who can blame them, with the stresses many people have to face? Saying that it just is impossible because of regulations and procedures is an easy way of controlling the pressure, for everyone's benefit. It might be easy but is it good practice? Clients, even aggressive and demanding ones, have the right to be told the truth about why they cannot have what they want. They should know if they fall outside the criteria for rationing a service. If they do not understand why they have been refused, they might not apply the next time when they could meet the criteria and be entitled to the service. They have no chance to modify their behaviour or improve their circumstances so that they might qualify. Instead, they will say: 'Oh well, they're just bureaucrats; there's no point in asking them.' At this point a member of the public is not getting his or her rights as a citizen. This reaction adds to the reputation of social workers and all public servants being bureaucrats and this helps no one.

For example, I once worked for a local authority which I suppose would now be called 'old Labour'. The councillors were very close to their constituents; they met them in the working men's club most nights of the week. People would come up to them and ask after their housing repairs, or the new flat for their daughter who was having a baby and so on. And what are councillors for? To get things for their constituents, naturally, as the constituents saw it. But the councillor and my colleague the housing manager who put up with most of this kind of pressure had the answer: there was a strict system of housing allocation by priority points and a wait-your-turn priority list for repairs.

In another authority I know, which I suppose you would describe as 'new Conservative', many majority councillors are local small businessmen. They are used to doing 'deals' in their business life; that is how they see the world. Their friends run into them at the health club or some such place and suggest it would be helpful if only the council would . . . that kind of thing. But again, they, the local government officers, have the answer: the rules are inflexible, even if they feel inclined to do the deal.

As we have seen though, the problem with inflexible rules is that it is difficult dealing with a situation that requires flexibility. Councillors and officers need skill, education and training in recognising when flexibility is required and what kind of flexibility they should use. Then, the organisation's system must administer and support appropriate discretion. We have failed to achieve that in British local government, and consequently we also do not have it in the British social services which are mainly part of local government. The purpose of this book is to argue that we should move in the direction of greater (appropriate) flexibility, to show how we should do it and to suggest that there are signs that the movement is beginning.

Bureaucratic behaviour: this book's topic and argument

Anyone who works in government, indeed anyone who works in a formal organisation, recognises the need for rules and obeying them. Nevertheless, as in the Macmillan's case, the rules sometimes do not meet the need for flexibility on behalf of the people we serve. Then, we are called 'bureaucratic' – a term implying insult. Bureaucratic behaviour raises problems for both sides: it is frustrating and difficult both for workers and for members of the public. If both sides recognise it as a problem, why does it remain so? This is because much of the academic analysis of 'bureaucracy' does not have this implication of inappropriate inflexibility. In sociology it is not necessarily an insult. Jacques (1990) argues, for example, that tasks are less or more complex, and that it is not a smooth transition from one to the other: there are sudden steps up in the level of complexity. The same applies, he says, when we consider mental work and accountability. So grades or layers occur almost naturally in organisations. He also argues that, in a complex organisation, accountability in a hierarchy is the only way of being completely clear about who is responsible for what. The academic analysis recognises the validity of having rules for accountability in an organisation, and many members of the public recognise the value of this too. Sometimes, however, the inflexibility of organising accountability in this way is inappropriate in any organisation, and, I argue, particularly in social work organisations. We all approve of the accountability but we dislike the inflexibility that results.

I have started in this Chapter from the experience that workers and the public have of inflexibility. I have suggested that this is inherent in the accountability systems of large organisations. In Chapter 2, I go further, and suggest that it is a particular problem at the moment because of important social changes. Changes in how people expect government to behave respond to social movements which accept greater diversity of people, ways of living and therefore social responses to that. However, government and large organisations have not changed so fast. Moreover, in the 1980s, we have experienced a period in which a particular political perspective, from the new Right, has combined with global economic changes to press government to operate in new ways. These political views imply greater control of government activity to achieve greater freedom in a market. However, trying to control government workers' behaviour does not sit well with trying to achieve a more open and flexible way of living through the market. The attempt to achieve greater market freedom will add to the social movements which have led to greater diversity and demands for flexible behaviour and practice. Consequently, the attempt both to control government employees and promote freedom is inconsistent and leads to confusion and conflicts.

So how do we, as bureaucrats and as social workers, deal with this inconsistency and conflict? This book explores the topic in two different ways. First, the early part of the book (Chapters 1 and 2) examines different aspects of the critique of social work as over-bureaucratic. This chapter looks at the idea of bureaucracy and bureaucratic behaviour; the next looks at the modern issue of managerialism. My argument is that over-bureaucratic behaviour is rightly criticised from both within social work and from outside. It is inappropriate for all government employees, but particularly for social workers, because I think they have a special role inherent in their work to combat bureaucracy. If social work becomes anti-bureaucratic, it faces the conflicts and inconsistencies of present trends particularly strongly. In these first two chapters I try to examine what is happening and look at some explanations for it. The next part of the book (Chapters 3 and 4) looks at different ways in which we might try to overcome some of the problems of social workers being over-bureaucratic. The final Chapter returns to the conflicts and social movements and changes. It looks at how social work and its role in society needs to change to deal with these trends.

All books have a point of view and this is the argument that I want to make. First, as I have already stated, I accept the validity of systems for accountability in formal organisations. Secondly, however, I think the value of inflexibility in those systems of accountability is overstated. I have been making the case for openness about criteria and how they are applied: there are many other related points detailed in Chapters 3 and 4. Thirdly, one of the special roles of social work in society is to overcome the problems of inflexibility in organisations on behalf of clients. Techniques for doing so are an integral aspect of social work values, knowledge and skill: we should foster and develop them. Fourthly, therefore, we have a particular responsibility not to become inflexible in our own organisations and this we have not been achieving very well. Fifthly, social work is not one of the professions which can operate totally on a basis of individual practitioner responsibility. It is as a profession bound up in playing organisational roles. Lastly therefore, looking to the 21st century, we have a responsibility to recast the relationship between social work and the organisations in which it operates. In Chapter 2, I call this the 'organisational settlement'. We should do this so that, as individuals, we can accept and play out our anti-bureaucratic role effectively. This would benefit both our clients and the organisations and societies that we serve. We also need, collectively, to reorganise the social services and social work to do so and Chapter 5 argues why and how we need to develop our practice and our professional and agency organisation to do so.

Arguments for bureaucracy

When an individual does something on their own behalf in their own way, it is quite clear who is 'responsible' for what happens – the individual. I have put 'responsible' in inverted commas because one question we need to look at is precisely what responsibility means – I shall come back to that later. First let us turn to what happens when more than one individual is involved in an act. If we want to see who is responsible, we have to divide responsibility among the people involved. It may be that one has responsibility and the others none, but often more than one person has different kinds or different amounts of responsibility. An 'organisation' is a social structure which makes formal such divisions between the responsibility of people who act together. We talk of an organisation where relationships among an identifiable group of people have been formally established to achieve defined purposes and goals. In an organisation, there are rules of behaviour and formal divisions of status marked by lines of communication and authority (Silverman, 1970, pp 8–14). However, there is no clear boundary between social structures of relationships which are within organisations and those which are not. Morgan (1997) proposes that organisations can be understood in different ways according to the metaphors we use to describe them. He suggests that they may be seen for example as sets of political relationships in which power is negotiated. Bureaucracies are usually described as being like 'machines', made up of many parts which fit together to make a working whole.

'Bureaucracy' is a description of a system of organising accountability within an organisation. It assumes that there is one source of authority in the organisation, from which comes the power to act on behalf of the organisation. Weber (Gerth and Mills, 1948, pp 196-244), the classic sociological source of the analysis, describes it as a form of authority and contrasts it with 'charismatic' authority. To understand 'bureaucracy', therefore, we have to know what 'authority' means. It is a complicated idea, and many books have been written about it. However, basically it means legitimated power: the capacity to get other people

6

to do something that they might not want to do (power). The person with power is accepted as being entitled to have this capacity (legitimated). To go a little further, the acceptance may come from various sources. For example, the law may confer power to require us to do something, or we may accept various kinds of moral authority. If we are religious, for example, we might accept that our priest has authority to require us to behave in certain ways. Charismatic authority, on the other hand, derives from the personality of the source of authority. Thus, a very attractive and interesting manager might be able to get us to do things that a more boring one could not. As well as being a theory of authority, Weber's work is also a theory of action. That is, he is concerned with how things are done and not only with structures in the abstract.

Outlining this distinction probably makes it obvious why bureaucracy is a common way of organising authority. It is commonplace because it creates certainty and the power can be clarified and backed up by sanctions, given by the law or custom. The power should also be used neutrally, according to law, custom and regulation. So bureaucracy has certainty, clarity and neutrality. We cannot all rely on being or having exciting and interesting 'charismatic' bosses. So to make sure things get done consistently, a system like bureaucracy is likely to be more effective. Modern ideas of bureaucracy as a way of managing organisations were developing around the same time as 'scientific management'; these alternative views of organisations and management as planned and rational are related. However, such models have existed for as long as history. They are particularly associated with armies, churches and the ancient empires of the Sumerians, Egyptians and Romans where many early forms of management developed.

One alternative to planning and management of human activity through rational means such as bureaucracy is to allow everyone to pursue their own interests, and the things that need to get done will be sorted out by negotiation. This is the idea behind the market and leads to individualism. It says that if everyone is free to pursue their own interests, the market will sort out what is most important. If people really want something, it is assumed that they will make more effort to do it themselves. Alternatively, they might pay more for getting it done and this will motivate others more to get it done. We shall be looking at some of the problems with this sort of idea in Chapter 2. Just for now it is relevant to say that at least some things might get done better or quicker if they are planned or if people cooperated in doing them. Also, markets need a mechanism to stop people pursuing their interests to the detriment of other people, for example, by stealing resources. Consequently, at least some things might need forms of authority to get them done. Most people, even if they strongly support market forms of organisation or rampant individualism, would accept that this is true of at least some things. The classic examples are defence and policing. These examples are apposite here because social services and social work are at least partly a form of social policing.

How is bureaucracy organised? The basic system is hierarchical. In a simple hierarchy (Figure 1.1) we have one superior and two subordinates. The superior has the authority to divide up the tasks of the organisation and direct the subordinates in parts of the task. Otherwise, superiors would have to do all the tasks. In a more complex hierarchy (Figure 1.2), there are more layers of authority, but the process is the same. The person at the top of the hierarchy has the ultimate authority. This permits them to command certain parts of the job to be given to subordinates, who also parcel out the tasks to their subordinates and so on down the line. In fact, this is sometimes called 'line' management, because a line of authority runs from the person with the ultimate authority to any subordinate in the organisation. Figure 1.2, by the way, shows a very even hierarchy with the same numbers of subordinates in each branch of the organisation. Usually different branches have different numbers of staff and they may be organised in more complex ways.

A bureaucracy, then, divides up tasks among the people available to do them, defines the tasks and defines which person in the hierarchy does which task. It also provides the authority to carry out their tasks, which a superior gives, ultimately on the authority of the person at the top. Bureaucracies, therefore, not only divide up authority but also create a division of labour. Theoretically, authority to act goes with the responsibility to undertake the specific tasks. One criticism of particular organisations sometimes is that they are not so good at giving out the responsibility or the resources to go with the tasks that they are only to eager to hand out. An important point, made by Jacques (1990), is that although bureaucracy and hierarchy obviously create a system of organisation, one reason that it persists is that it makes employment of individuals possible. This is because it defines individual accountability, so it must always be seen individually, as I have described it. Since employees are always employed individually, group accountability is very hard to organise.

Figure 1.1 A simple hierarchy

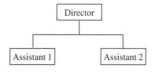

Figure 1.2 A complex hierarchy

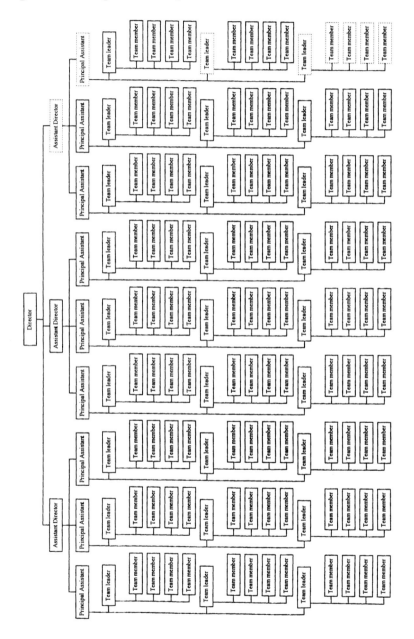

Bureaucracies can make all this work because, according to Weber (Gerth and Mills, 1948), they are based on rules, established by the ultimate authority, often derived from the law. Everyone is accountable for following the rules. This leads to administrative systems, regulations, guidance about practice and similar arrangements. The bureaucratic system breaks down unless the rules are followed, so actions and decisions are conditioned by rule-following, rather than by creative thought.

Some of the problems with this will be obvious. It will all be very clear, but only if the tasks can be defined and responsibility and authority allocated appropriately. If the tasks are indefinable, discretion must also be allocated, and then it becomes more complicated to allocate authority and responsibility. Also, this will work well where the tasks are stable. Where there is frequent change, it will be complicated to keep on reallocating tasks and responsibilities as things change. In a well-known study, Burns and Stalker (1966) showed that some organisations in some environments can be quite successful as bureaucracies. They called these mechanistic organisations. Others were in environments or had tasks which involved a lot of change, and needed to have a more flexible way of doing things (organic organisations). Social work is a task which frequently requires that kind of flexibility and operates in a changing environment. Therefore, to carry out social work successfully, organic organisations could be more effective. Among other things, these recognise that informal relationships and structure in organisations are just as important for getting things done as formal structure.

Another problem lies in guiding everything by the rules. Where bureaucracies have to deal with complexities, rules are adapted. One of the most common ways of doing this is by incorporating professional discretion within bureaucratic organisations. Mintzberg (1979) suggests that in a professional bureaucracy, professionals are trained in standardised tasks and operate with considerable autonomy. The standardised training means that the certainty and consistency of bureaucracies are maintained. However, the flexibility of the professionals' autonomy makes what would otherwise be an unreasonably restrictive work pattern satisfactory.

At present, social services organisations are like this pattern with social workers in particular operating as 'bureau-professionals'. This is because they often act as the gatekeepers for access to many resources, and make most of the discretionary professional decisions about clients. The crucial issues in a professional bureaucracy are concerned with how relations between the bureaucratic system and the professionals are regulated. As we shall see in Chapter 2, the pattern of these relationships has been changing in the 1980s, through the imposition of managerial philosophies in a way which is unhelpful. However, Mintzberg (1979) also proposes that many modern organisations have developed as 'adhocracy' in which shifting workgroups work on *ad hoc* projects. Most public social services agencies are not like this, although some voluntary organisations might approach it. Clearly, however, it is possible to conceive of organisations working in flexible arenas where formal structure becomes less important. My argument in this book suggests that external pressures will force social services organisations to become more like this. As a result, their structure and management will have to change .

What is responsibility and accountability?
Now I return to something I left out of the discussion above. It is: what do we mean by 'responsibility'? Following on from that, I have sometimes used the word 'accountability'. Is that the same thing as 'responsibility' or does is it means something different, even if it is connected with 'responsibility'?

The distinction that I usually make, and that I think many people mean when they talk about responsibility, is that it is a personal feeling. We feel responsible for something if we have accepted that it is for us to take on doing it, and that other people are entitled to blame us if it is not done. Accountability is a bit more than that. It involves responsibility which is accepted by us or applied to us on behalf of an organisation. So the organisational structure we are involved in mediates the responsibility and it relates only to our role within the organisation. We often say, for example: 'I'm not responsible for that.' What we mean by this statement is that we do not feel responsible, because the organisation would not hold us accountable. Alternatively, we sometimes say, rather apologetically: 'I feel responsible for that', meaning that although we realise the organisation would not hold us accountable, we nevertheless feel our responsibility.

On the other hand, we can know we are accountable in our job role, but not feel responsible outside it. This enables us to sleep at night and only worry about our work at work: we accept the accountability there, but the feeling does not always translate into our private feelings. Of course, sometimes accountability and responsibility overlap. Then, we worry about our work at home, or we feel responsible for something because we like to do a good job and our accountability sets off feelings of responsibility.

This means that our emotional response to a situation sometimes enforces accountability: we are accountable because we *feel* responsible. However, this is not always so, and it may not be so for everyone all the time. Sometimes, in my job, when I have not been feeling good about my organisation, I feel less emotionally responsible for what I know my employer will hold me accountable for. Occasionally, I have not bothered too much about making sure the records are in order, while I would take considerable trouble to see that a client feels satisfied. So, we can ask: what does accountability mean if we do not have the accompanying feelings of responsibility?

The word 'accountability' implies the duty to render an account to someone to show that we have done something that we ought to have done. In a bureaucracy, accountability is often managed by written reports and records. Weber (Gerth and Mills, 1948, p 197) proposes that reference to 'the files' as the basis for certainty and consistency in an organisation is a defining characteristic of a bureaucracy.

Different kinds of accountability that exist include the following:

- The duty to *report*. This is the essence of rendering an account – we have to tell someone what has happened, sometimes in a structured way. For example, if we were accountants, we might have to provide financial accounts of income and expenditure or assets and liabilities. As social workers, we might have to go back to someone to say what we have done about a case. This might take place under supervision and might be a spoken account. Alternatively, we might have to write a case record or provide a written report or assessment. This aids accountability, because we limit our behaviour to things that we would be happy to report.

- The duty to *explain*. This goes further. Sometimes, we not only have to say what happened but show why it happened that way rather than in some other possible way. For accountants, this often leads to 'notes to the accounts' which say how the income is made up, or analyse what the expenditure was paid out for. As social workers, we might have to say why we decided that Mrs Whiting should not have a care package, or why we are arguing that Benny Birch should be looked after by the local authority child care service. This aids accountability because we think more carefully about what we do, if we have to explain why we did it.

- The duty to *judge and assess*. A little step further is to make a judgment about our explanation. We look at a situation and say that we think someone is at risk or that they need a service, and we collect the evidence to support that judgement (or we could provide it if we were asked). Related to that is our assessment, which is an overall judgment about the situation and which considers the consequences of our judgements for future decision-making. Sometimes this takes place within a formal structure of decision-making, such as a community care assessment or a financial assessment for a charge. Also, we use 'assessment' to describe the examination of a variety of circumstances affecting a client or service: we reflect critically on it and come to a view about its value or success or make recommendations for the future.

- The duty to *justify*. Justification is a step beyond explaining and judging why something happened. Here, we present evidence and argument that it was right or appropriate that it happened or why we did what we did which caused it to happen.

- The duty to accept *blame or praise and its consequences*. On top of a duty to justify, we may have to accept blame for something that went wrong, or praise if it went right. Blame or praise might also lead to consequences. For example, if we fail to do something really serious or if we are failing a lot of the time, we might be disciplined or lose our job. Such actions are formal, organisational structures for allocating blame. Alternatively, if we are doing really well we might get extra pay or promotion. For example, applications for new jobs or promotion are more likely to be successful if we have been doing well in the present job.

Since there are different kinds of accountability, it follows that different meanings are attached to statements about accountability. In ordinary life, the different meanings can be quite unclear. Sometimes accountability is a 'your-job-is-in-danger' type of duty, sometimes it is an 'I'd-like-you-to-tell-me-what's-going-on' type. Sometimes different meanings of accountability are combined as elements in a composite view of accountability. The difference arises not only in different situations, but also with different kinds of people. Very often, high-status professionals are given considerable freedom and dis-cretion to make judgements. The consequence is that when their judgements are seriously wrong, their professional standing or their right to work at all is in jeopardy, because they have been given that freedom.

In this list of the elements or types of accountability, I have referred to 'duty'. What is this duty and where does it come from? One origin of the duty lies in the employment of a worker and his or her contract of employment or, for a freelance, service contract. So the duty comes from contract law: if you agree to something, the law makes you do what you agreed to or you suffer the consequences.

In organisations, there is another source of duty which comes from the authority divided up within the structure of the organisation. If it is a local authority (notice the word here: 'authority' – the whole basis of the organisa-tion is the legitimation of power) the duty is imposed by the authority of the councillors which in turn comes from their democratic election. Similarly in the central civil service, the government is elected and this gives them the authority to impose their will to get things done. In private or voluntary sector organisa-tions, the authority comes from the 'association' of people who formed the company or organisation (many voluntary organisations are also companies). When they get together to form the organisation, they agree (for a company) to a 'memorandum and articles of association' or (more simply) a 'constitution'. These state the objectives for which the company or association is formed, and the law enforces these. The company or association cannot do things which are not in their constitution. The authority to employ people to get the job done comes from elective authority or from the constitution of the organisation. Therefore, the contract of employment includes acceptance of the authority of the elective body or constitution.

Political and social origins of bureaucratic behaviour

If bureaucratic behaviour is such a problem, why does it persist? And why is it a problem now? My answer to these questions is that bureaucratic behaviour is inherent in British political and social systems. I have suggested that there are advantages to bureaucracy which have encouraged its persistence in many organisations: certainty, neutrality, clarity in decision-making and in defining people's jobs were the main points. However, particular disadvantages have accumulated in British government. The British approach to public services is particularly centralised, authoritarian, legalistic and non-pluralistic. It has become more so in the last two decades. As Hague *et al.*,(1998, p. 180), in an authoritative politics text, put it:

> *In most of Western Europe, local government has a higher status than in the new world . . . [reflecting] the European doctrine of subsidiarity – the idea that matters should be dealt with at local level whenever possible. In a European context, English local government is the great exception . . . English councils are . . . protected neither by provincial governments (Britain is a unitary state), nor by constitutional entrenchment (Britain lacks a codified constitution), nor by the power of general competence (councils can only do what central government explicitly permits) . . . England's local authorities were reduced to virtual servant status by 18 years of assertive Conservative rule beginning in 1979. Over this period, British government centralised at a time when many European democracies were devolving it. No wonder Britain declined to support the European Charter of Local Self-Government, adopted by the Council of Europe in 1985.*

I have come to share this view partly because of my experience in Nordic countries. In fact I am writing at the moment looking out over the snowy roofs of Helsinki, courtesy of the Swedish Institute of Social Science at the University of Helsinki. Let me tell you about some of those experiences.

Shared and pluralist decision-making

Local authorities in Finland, and in most Nordic countries, are quite small, covering small populations. Hague *et al*. (1998, p. 181) show that English local authorities cover uniquely large populations. The Finnish planning process involves budget-setting which they do as part of the work of a strategic regional local authority. These budgets are then incorporated into planning for national budgets. But the idea that local authorities should have their spending directed by central government, as in Britain, is less true in Finland. They are completely different types of bodies; one is not superior to the other. Obviously the budget planning is negotiated and power and influence is exerted, so perhaps the result, budgetary constraint, is in the end rather similar. But the feeling of local freedom to decide is very different.

There are several aspects of life which connect with this – who can say what causes what? For one thing, local authorities are not really regarded as 'government'. Once, I started a lecture to a Finnish audience with what in Britain would be obvious: 'Most social workers are employed by government . . .' I got no further: 'Oh, I don't think that's true,' said a member of the audience. I knew that most Finnish social workers are employed by local authorities, so I enquired further. To my Finnish audience, government was 'central government.' Local councils, significantly I think, called *kommune*, were 'us', 'ours'; they were local, you knew the people involved; you rang them up.

Connected to this is the absence of the rule of *ultra vires*, which is a fundamental principle of British public administration. It establishes the principle that a public authority may only do what is expressly permitted or required by law, that is, by central government. A person, on the other hand, may do anything not expressly prevented by law. This means that in Britain, officials, including social workers, need to have a close concern for the legal and procedural aspects of their work. Even when it is not necessary, the convention affects the style and approach of the services. Not so in Nordic countries. Communes are there to do what is required in their area. If they think they need to do something, then of course that is what they should do. The idea that they would have to wait for an Act of Parliament is incomprehensible. Social workers and members of the public can effect changes by lobbying their local representatives. Here again is the idea that local services are separate from government. Nordic people expect their local authority to provide for the needs that are present in their community rather than wait for an Act of Parliament which says what they should do. They expect flexibility in budgets to make the provision that is necessary.

Would this be realistic in the British situation? The present situation is a political choice that the British electorates have made (although perhaps not very clearly). Nordic people pay a much higher proportion of their salaries in taxes, but on the whole they get a much more protective welfare state. The 'old Labour' local authority I once worked in during the 1970s took the same attitude. We had a very high level of provision. Frankly, at times we would have to cast around for people to receive our community services for elderly and disabled people. The British backed away from this kind of spending and provision in the 1980s and 1990s. It is perfectly possible therefore to have an alternative situation.

Bureaucratic behaviour and the public sector
There has also been a considerable critique of the efficiency of the public sector, which has focused to some extent on bureaucratic behaviour. People complain about the bureaucratic behaviour of public organisations, which they find frustrating and obstructive. They associate inflexible bureaucracy with state provision. Why is this, when there are many large private sector organisations which are organised bureaucratically? There are three reasons which I look at in this section. First, public sector organisations have more of a regulatory role, involving social control, than private sector organisations. Secondly, public sector organisations often provide services which are rationed, and limit choice for service users. Thirdly, there has generally been more investment in private sector organisations, which means they can use technology more effectively to provide better services.

The social services, and most public sector organisations to some extent, have a regulatory and social control role. Although many people accept this and recognise it has to be done, nobody likes having it done to them. People dislike, just as much, ticket control on the railways, safety requirements, heavy security and similar tasks done by private sector organisations. Public sector organisations take the brunt of this kind of work, and people experience them as controlling rather than enabling. Similarly, compared with private commercial organisations, which are there to provide what you want and as much as you want, public sector organisations have to limit what you can have. They have all sorts of rules about applications, and all sorts of checks on you when you apply. Compared with many commercial services, public sector provision seems obstructive about giving you what you want. Many people have the same feelings about commercial organisations, like banks, which have requirements before you can use their services. They understand it but they dislike it. Finally, because of poor investment, many public sector organisations may not

16

have the best equipment, technology or facilities in their offices and services. They often feel run-down; buildings are not properly maintained; service is slow. Everybody accepted that British Rail was run-down, because it was government funded; they are less prepared to accept it of the privatised railways.

Compared with their experience of a rapidly improving and service-oriented private sector, many peoples' experience of the public sector, for the above reasons, is unfavourable. For many years of the Conservative government, this was explained as one of the consequences of public ownership; state services were naturally inferior. Many people know this is not right, but this continuous critique of the public sector has had its impact on the public image. Slowness, difficulty, differences of role are put down to 'bureaucracy' and compare unfavourably with very different services in the commercial world. Even if we took the time and trouble to explain it to members of the public, it is quite likely that this would look like special pleading and excuses. Bureaucracy, then, is associated with the public sector, probably inevitably, because of its role and functions.

Regulation and fairness
The role of law and regulation is, therefore, part of the reason for the association of British public services with bureaucratic behaviour. However, it does not have to be like that, because British social work has an exceptionally strong concern for legality and procedure rather than for discretion. Conversations with Nordic social workers suggest that their work is guided by the law, but they do not have a daily concern for its limitations and requirements. People expect them to do what is best and on the whole accept their judgements about what to do.

A Swedish colleague, having heard something about it, asked me how quality assurance was being implemented in British social services. He listened to my description of the social services inspectorate, joint reviews with the Audit Commission, residential care home registration, foster care and pre-school day care registers with mounting incredulity. In the end, he shook his head and said: 'You British. You cannot just leave anyone to get on with their work. As soon as you have something, you have to inspect it and regulate it and control it.' Similarly, a German colleague was outraged by the idea that in Britain a government agency and employers' organisations had influence over the curriculum for social work education. To him, this was an attack on a basic constitutional right to academic freedom. This was rather important to him – Germany and many other countries have had recent experience of what happens when government is ceded the right to control everything.

Now, I do not say that the British system is wholly wrong. Most Nordic countries have small fairly homogeneous populations and do not have the range of conflicts of interest that exist in British cities. Small scale means that there can be a local awareness of problems: this is replaced by various regulatory and inspectorial systems in Britain. Hence, I think, the reliance on 'we would negotiate', responsiveness and openness just would not do in a more complex and heterogeneous Britain. The style of approach is different in Nordic countries: rather egalitarian and pluralist. No one would think of enforcing a centralised government policy agenda on each local authority, although there is an expectation that a local authority would be following the best professional trends to meet the needs of their people. Some do not, and have what professionals would regard as rather conservative and limited provision. The consequence may be a variation in the quality of services and a lack of rigour. Along with this, though, comes a sense of involvement and shared responsibility between public and officialdom which the British rather struggle to achieve.

On the other hand, I think I would rather have the British social worker's constant awareness of and focus on service users' legal rights. These have come from stricter legal controls over professional discretion. Also, the range and sophistication of British social and other public services is hard to provide in smaller communities with fewer resources. I would also rather have the pluralist British private and voluntary sectors, and active, rather confrontational, interest groups representing service users, which barely exist and are more heavily involved in the professional services in most Nordic countries. There, pluralism exists in the variety of political parties and their policies, and the negotiation processes which go on to create policies within government.

Political and media style and structure
In Britain, however, there is still mainly a two-party system, where coalitions and negotiations go on within the parties which contain widely different points of view. Attempts to change those internal coalitions are made to respond to new pressures. In the 1990s, much of this seems to be around greater involvement in the European Union. It is not clear yet whether this will lead to a realignment of political parties. There are also constitutional changes which may lead to greater pluralism outside the present two-party system, particularly in Northern Ireland, Scotland and Wales, where local parties have strong influence. Because of the strains inherent in the political party's internal coalitions, greater importance is given in the British system to political control. Greater involvement in the European Union and growing pluralism arising from the new country assemblies in Britain would lead to a much wider range of political influences than what we experience at the moment.

18

One characteristic of these internal political coalitions is the need for control of expressions of dissent. In the British system it is ideally handled internally rather than brought out into the open. One consequence is a secrecy about official information that in Nordic countries or the USA would border on the paranoid. Arising from this is the way the press and other information media behave. They seek evidence of hidden information and divisions because this enables hidden debates and issues to come to the surface. This leads to a much more conflictual and intrusive press than some other countries' experience. This has consequences for political style. Things which go wrong are pursued as 'gaffes' at least and sometimes as 'disasters'. Therefore, local government administration is concerned with avoiding anything which might be criticised in this unreasonable and aggressive way. Where broader political differences are represented in a range of political parties, openness inevitably brings these issues to the surface. Because this happens a lot in more pluralist political systems, there is not so much invested in a particular policy. In any case policy might have to be negotiated in a coalition. As a consequence, social workers would be able to have some political influence to achieve changes they desire within and through different political parties. The main focus of lobbying at present focuses heavily on behind-the-scenes influence on officials. This is less open than direct political debate and coalition.

These political characteristics of Britain also have their impact on government and its officials. Achieving policy goals which can be differentiated from those of the opposing party has become increasingly important to British political parties. More negotiated and flexible outcomes cannot be easily represented in the political and media environment which expects conflict over policy goals. Equally, administrative and management problems are represented as political failures to which blame is attached. It might be better to see them as issues to be resolved and evidence of need or opportunity to make progress. This encourages the endemic secrecy of British government and administration. It is important not to go to extremes. The media play a very important role in Britain in identifying and pursuing people's rights and government failures. What we are concerned with here is the consequence of a procedural culture and a style of always having to justify yourself to the press.

Other social issues

We must also think about the influence of social class. One reason for the style of Nordic politics and administration is the homogeneity of Nordic populations. This is not only in the relatively low level (except in Sweden) of ethnic diversity compared with Britain, but also in the lower importance given to class divisions. An aristocracy and royal families are less significant in Nordic countries. Also, civil society, that collection of social influences and groupings, is more diverse and egalitarian. All countries have groups who are excluded from full participation in their society and who are relatively powerless because of it. However, Britain seems to have the remnants of a class system which allies social divisions with social exclusions in a particularly powerful way. There are people with power, particularly at the national level, who have had privileged education and advantages in preferment which adversely affect anyone who is different from the 'white male' stereotype.

Bureaucratic organisation and behaviour backs up those social exclusions, because, as we have seen, it is fundamentally hierarchical. Where class hierarchies are important, organisational hierarchies will tie social exclusions to organisational exclusions. We all know that a southern accent, being male and having an educated form of speech gets us listened to. Being female, having regional or ethnic minority accents and evidence of poor education often excludes people from consideration. We are immediately aware of social difference, and stereotypes go with this awareness. Foreign visitors often find the British awareness of origins and class through accent and behaviour bizarre and old-fashioned.

The argument: bureaucratic behaviour is unnecessary

To sum up what I have been saying, British local authorities in which most social workers are employed have a particular style and structure. The way it is established and that it gives authority for administrative and professional action derived from politically-originated policy creates that style. British local government has a very clear distinction between politicians and officers, including professionals employed in local government. The politicians set policy and budgets, influenced by senior professionals, and the officers put it into effect, involving politicians acting on behalf of their constituents from time to time. This encourages rule-following and compliance, because actions have to be justified by their compliance to law, regulation and political policy. This is reinforced by an aggressively critical media and longstanding class and social divisions and stereotypes. Is this a necessary way of organising the social services?

Experience of working in a voluntary organisation points up these characteristics of British local government. The social divisions are the same, but the political and administrative structures are less marked. One of the great shocks for me moving from local government to the voluntary sector was the way in which the management committee did not see themselves as responsible for setting policy. They might have accepted responsibility for identifying a basic philosophy or mission, approving and being informed about policy. However, they expected me to come up with the ideas about what we should do and how we should do it. I know this sense of shock is shared by many people who move from the state to the voluntary sector. That sense of political control just disappears. Even where the management committee has a very clear policy and style, for example, in women's refuges, they usually recruit staff who have the same philosophy. So there is a much greater sense of shared policy-making and practice development in the voluntary sector.

Similarly, having worked in local government, I was surprised in the voluntary sector, even in quite large organisations, by the flexibility about money and payments. The first time I put in my expenses in a voluntary sector organisation, I expected a computer-generated payment a month or two in the future, as in local government. I was astonished when the accountant came down from upstairs and handed over the cash about half an hour later. Yet that organisation was administered to tight financial controls. Accounting was to a very high standard. However, cash was paid when it was appropriate. In the voluntary sector, a senior finance manager trained in the private sector once said to me, as I was looking at budgets: 'The reason for having money is to spend it on the things we're here to do. My job is not to hold on to the money. It's to make sure the money's fully spent on the right things that the committee wants to do.'

There are three reasons for the difference between local government and voluntary sector controls. They are: political control of policy, the rationing role and the requirement for fairness in certain expenditure decisions. On the first point, budgets set the wherewithal to comply with the policies of the local authority. That is the reason that virement (moving money from one budget head to another) by officers is strictly controlled in government; it represents a shift in the political decision-making. Related to that, political control leads to hierarchy and the lack of shared working between politicians and officers in most local authorities which is present in voluntary organisations and other countries. On the rationing role, we have already seen that government responsibility for rationing services and expenditure means a tightness of spending controls. This secures both fairness and the ability to justify that every expenditure is appropriate. Similarly, on fairness, when local authorities are assessing for limited services, such as community care provision, people expect rigorous policy control so that everyone is treated the same. Territorial justice, as it is called, across the country is also expected though it is difficult to deliver. This is why Nordic social workers would not accept that their organisations are non-bureaucratic in spite of the picture I have presented. They are responsible for administering much of the social security system. This is as bounded by procedural rules and legal rights and duties as the British system is, and makes them feel very much like bureaucrats.

I have tried to show that bureaucratic behaviour, as we find it in the British social services, is not an inevitable way of going on. It is a consequence of our government and political system, backed up by our social assumptions. There are benefits to bureaucracy which justify keeping some of its features. However, a much more open, pluralist and flexible system of political decision-making might well mitigate some of these problems. More flexibility could easily be accommodated in an equally well-controlled policy-making and administrative structure. This is successful elsewhere.

Related to that, I have suggested that procedural and inflexible decision-making in public sector services has justifications, but that it is possible to imagine alternatives. The fundamental alternative is to develop a greater degree of discretion for workers in the public sector. Consequently, a system of administration is needed which gives authority and support to the reasonable exercise of discretion and flexibility. The purpose of this book is to argue that, in the future, we should try to achieve this in the British social services.

However, before going on to look at what we might do to develop greater flexibility and less bureaucratic behaviour in the social services, we need to examine another issue in local government and political administration: the political and organisational issue of managerialism.

Chapter 2.
MANAGERIALISM

'Independence for social work': the cry of the 1960s

Social workers have often thought it important that their most senior managers have done social work themselves. *Social Work Today* was published by the British Association of Social Workers as its journal from 1970 until 1994. For its first two years or so, Jef Smith wrote a column about the appointments of the first directors of social services. At the same time, the Association pressurised local authorities to appoint people with social work qualifications and experience to be directors of social services. Going back even further, a predecessor journal, *Case Conference*, recounts over many months, a dispute with a London Borough about its refusal to appoint a social worker as its Children's Officer. This led to its being listed by social work associations as a place where social workers should not apply for jobs. At the time, Scottish local authorities were required to appoint a qualified social worker to directorships of social work. Similarly, English local authorities had to have the shortlists for directorships approved by the relevant government ministry. Hall's (1976) account of the Seebohm reorganisation of social work in the 1970s shows how social workers campaigned for independence successfully. They were fighting against a strong lobby from 'medical officers of health' (local authority doctors: the group who are now often called 'community physicians') that doctors should take charge of social work and run the new social services departments, integrated into local authority health departments.

What was all this about? This period was, I would say, the higher-water mark of the movement for the professionalisation of social work in Britain. Social workers were asserting very forcefully that social work was a distinctive activity, different from other related professional activities. They argued that it should be increasingly regarded as a profession, independent from other professions. Therefore, social work decisions should only be taken by social workers, because if social work is a profession, it would have a distinctive knowledge, value and skill base. Only social workers could say whether this had been properly applied. It follows from this that only social workers can manage social work, assessing decisions from the same knowledge, value and skill base.

The aim of this movement was independence for social work from domination by the decisions of other professions. It also asserted the significance of the difference between social work and medical decisions or the decisions of other professions. There might be disputes about whether social work is an independent 'profession' – it depends what 'profession' means. However, the reality is of a separate occupational group in a strong position in a major local government department. This group has social functions which are a major aspect of the state in Britain and which are present in the societies of most other countries.

Another issue concerned people about 'being a profession'. Some occupational groups who are traditionally regarded as professions have a model of 'individual practitioner responsibility'. This means that the practitioner is responsible for the decisions which relate to their professional work. The organisation of work in those professions was historically arranged to protect and enhance that individual practitioner responsibility. So the local priest decides on the appropriate things to say in sermons, and how and whether to provide pastoral care to people in the congregation. The doctor holds 'clinical responsibility' for decisions about patients and the lawyer works in a collegial partnership where each individual is responsible for professional practice. They all comply with codes of practice and ethics, their professions have support and checking mechanisms, requirements for training, and they often have advisors and management systems surrounding them. But the actual professional decisions are theirs alone to take, and if they go wrong, their relationship is with a professional hierarchy, rather than an organisation. Very often, people assume that to be a profession this is how it has to work.

However, the pressures of the age alter individual professional responsibility in modern times. Priests work in hierarchies and their employment mostly follows the rules of formal employment by an organisation, so they become like voluntary organisation workers. Most doctors are surrounded by complex management and accountability systems in hospitals and health organisations. In most countries (the USA excepted) they work in some way for the state, and as part of multiprofessional teams. In this way, they are beholden to political decisions and other professionals' influences in resources and organisation. Increasingly, lawyers work in fairly large organisations, with specialisation. In all cases, consumer organisations, complaints procedures and social pressures have limited the autonomy that individual professionals can have. In many other professions, professionals are employed to do complex jobs in large private and public organisations. Such professionals must comply with management systems and the legal requirements of their employers. Accountants, architects, engineers, nurses, psychologists, teachers and many more: all these are accepted as professionals and gain, in carrying out their expert jobs, a great deal of autonomy in decision-making. However, they are also part of organisational structures and systems for accountability to non-professional bodies.

So the form and management of individual practitioner accountability are changing, and the constraints on it are considerable. It is a misunderstanding to maintain that social work is not a profession because it is part of organisations and workers do not have complete individual professional responsibility. We have to understand autonomy and responsibility in a more complex way.

So, in the modern situation new areas of controversy over professionalisation arise. Autonomy and professionalisation in social work are in conflict with newer forces: managerialism and consumerism. In this Chapter, I explore both these trends and the impact they have on bureaucratisation in social work. I argue that they are particularly relevant to social work, because the nature of social work in Britain causes these developments to bear on it particularly strongly.

Managerialism
Managerialism comes from the idea that management is an activity informed by its own knowledge, skills and values. In this view, management is itself a profession, separate and different from the activity which is being managed and the knowledge, skills and values which inform it. It follows from this that the structures, processes and activities of management have their own logic and character. Accepting this idea implies believing that management is something other than social work. Consequently, managers would not need to be able to do social work to manage it. The claim is that a manager can manage anything, without any need to understand the content of what they are managing.

This view of the autonomy and professional character of management has been growing up since the 1940s when the first management schools were set up. However, it has been transformed in the 1980s and 1990s by the major political impetus from the new Right of what Australians such as Rees (1991) and Ife (1997) call, 'economic rationalism'. In Britain and America this has become attached to personalities as 'Thatcherism' and 'Reaganomics'.

There are two factors in this transformation of managerialism: a particular view of the role of the state which derives from an economic philosophy and, building on that view, a political approach to the management of state services. Clarke and Newman (1997, ix) argue that the importance of managerialism from the 1980s onwards represents a new 'settlement' of relationships between the citizen and the state and between management and politics. They see three aspects of this settlement. One is a *political–economic* settlement between capitalism and the free market and between socialism and public provision of services through the state. Arising from this is a compromise between market-driven inequality and equality guaranteed through citizenship. The argument is that an accepted balance between these two factors in society changed, and we are settling on a new balance. Thatcherism in the 1980s threw it off balance; perhaps 'New Labour' represents a new balance. This might be less oriented towards the market than Thatcherism, but less oriented towards public provision of services than the 'postwar consensus' which was broadly agreed, before Thatcher.

Another aspect of the settlement is *social*. It represents a balance between themes of full male employment founded on families in which there is a 'patriarchal' and heterosexual division of labour creating a welfare state. This supports national unity and citizenship within it, because rights to welfare support are universal, provided the conditions of full male employment and the familial division of labour are maintained (Williams, 1992). The 'familial' division of labour is where mainly men work and women mainly manage the home and do domestic tasks and child care.

Finally there is an *organisational* settlement, which coordinates welfare provision through a balance between bureaucratic administration and professionalism. Bureaucracy supports, as we have seen in Chapter 1, social, political and personal certainty, clarity and neutrality, through administration by a system of formal rules. Professionalism, on the other hand offers flexibility achieved through the acceptance of some interventions based on expert judgement. These settlements were destroyed in Britain. First, economic weakness destroyed the political–economic settlement. This produced a political movement which argued that changes were needed which removed the possibility of economic equality, and which was even opposed in principle to equality. Then, social movements questioned the division of labour within families and supported diversity of family relationships. Part of this was in recognising and valuing disabled and gay and lesbian lifestyles. Also, some of this diversity came from the valuation of different family lifestyles in ethnic minority groups. These social and economic changes affected the organisational structure of public services which were challenged to respond to these changes.

One response to these challenges, from the new Right, was to reaffirm the economic and family values through the way state services were organised. Thus, social security and social welfare services were reorganised to emphasise economic and family responsibility. Against this, social pressures built up to recognise diversity and change. Most obviously, these pressures came through movements for equality between ethnic groups, gender equality and broader anti-discrimination. This implied a different approach to provision of services. In this way, public services became the battleground for the colliding forces of these movements. The New Right sought to transform public services and attain a different culture of service. In particular, it sought to displace the power of 'bureau-professional' relations. That is, this movement challenged the settlement in which established systems of rules were made flexible enough to deal with complex situations through professional judgements and in which professionals' discretion was accepted.

Pollitt (1993) offers the most comprehensive analysis of managerialism. He shows how scientific management developed from Taylorism. He sees it as a form of, or 'neo'- (a new manifestation of) Taylorism. Taylorism sees the essential purpose of management as *control*, and argues that control is best achieved by deciding levels of effort required to achieve whatever outcomes are wanted. Levels of effort are defined quantitatively as in the classic Taylorist technique, work study. When normal effort has been defined, greater effort is rewarded, again by quantitative means, that is, financial reward. So, in an office, how long it takes the average typist to type a letter of two hundred words is worked out. People who can do it faster receive higher pay. Achieving this permits moving away from control by relationships between manager and managed. Indeed it is essential, because rewards are given according to effort. This leads to techniques such as performance-related pay, and to a removal of general terms and conditions of service for employees. Instead, they must be dealt with according to local conditions reflecting the labour market. At first, in the public services in the 1980s, this approach led to a concern for cost-consciousness and performance indicators.

However, these management approaches were implemented in a dominant political environment of 'economic rationalism'. This philosophy proposes that the main route to progress lies in increasing economic productivity; to emphasise the point, progress is defined in economic terms and improvements in productivity define economic progress. Such progress comes from improvements in applying new technologies. So if preschool children are to make better progress, a more effective preschool curriculum must be introduced. Large, multifunctional organisations are the best social structures for achieving this. These include multinational corporations and large state agencies managed corporately, that is, managed so that all their policies and functions are consistent and support each other. This approach is sometimes called 'joined-up policy' or 'singing from the same hymn-sheet'. Thus, to improve preschool curricula, changes in social services (and possibly housing) departments may be needed so that they support the changes made in education. Part of this consistent policy approach is to ensure that the workforce is disciplined to achieve the corporate policy as productively as possible. To do this, effective management means that managers must have wide discretion to respond to local conditions, or be 'free to manage', as people sometimes say. This goes against profession-alism, because professionals' loyalty is to their specialisation rather than to corporate decisions. So, managerialism argues that social workers should not be paid on a fixed national scale, but should be paid according to managers' assessment of their achievements. The achievements required would be set by the national policy agenda rather than the workers' own judgements about the needs of their clients. This, managerialism argues, is the only way to ensure that they deliver the national policy agenda.

Pollitt (1993) argues that managerialism became important in response to postwar social trends. European countries established welfare states, relying on economic growth to maintain and develop social policies which supported the welfare of individuals and communities. Most government expenditure went on social issues soon after the war, and in the 1960s the USA caught up. Thus, social expenditure was rising. However, frequent swings in economic growth and recession led to increasing concern about whether growth could continue to provide for this expenditure. Increases in the population of elderly people and in single-parent families, mainly headed by women, led to pressure on social expenditure. The general child population dropped, leading to less need for schools expenditure. It was possible for governments of the 'new Right' in the 1980s to argue that economic development must have priority. To achieve this, social expenditure by the state must be curbed. Otherwise, the economy would not sustain it (pensions), or social change was needed to avoid dependency and (possibly) immorality (single parents), or there was scope for reduction (education). However, politically, the public were committed to maintaining state involvement in these services. Therefore, the new Right approach was to 'manage' these services more economically, and managerialist ideas provide a sympathetic approach to doing so.

For example, in community care, quasi-markets were introduced so that com-petition would stimulate better and cheaper provision. Social workers would assess people's needs for care, rather than, as previously, their being able to spend their own social security allowance to buy residential care. Thus, as Lewis and Glennerster's (1996) research shows, the government's main policy agenda was introducing markets and stopping rising residential care expendi-ture. This was successfully achieved. One way of doing this was to introduce the innovation of care management within social work practice. However, this was done in a confused and unclear way. It did not take up all the potential pro-fessional advantages of care management, because the 'economic management' priority interfered with the effective professional development of care management (Payne, 1995).

This is how managerialism, while not necessarily allied with new Right political philosophies or economic rationalism, became part of the new Right political programme. In turn, this led to privatisation, marketisation or contracting out of public services. This meant that, instead of running public services directly, state agencies offered contracts to non-public agencies to provide for their citizens. This led to a mixed economy in a market or quasi-market in which different types of organisations provide welfare services, instead of just one. Also, the focus of state services and benefits was tightened so that fewer gained access to them. Another move was to reduce provision, for example, by removing the connection between pensions increases and wage inflation. To achieve such measures, significant changes in management approach were required. As we have seen, within managerialist approaches to management, this implies a focus on control through quantification with such methods as performance-related pay.

Criticisms of managerialism

However, there are substantial criticisms of managerialism. Pollitt (1993, pp111–46) summarises them (and comments much more extensively than I do here) under 5 headings, as follows.

Lack of coherence and consistency
Managerialism's approach is internally inconsistent with the new 'joined-up' approach to policy-making in the way it views management control and in its approach to decentralisation for the following reasons.

Managerialism neglects motivating people in favour of control. Also, its approach to control is offering financial reward according to merit or effort, which is an ineffective motivator, particularly for public servants. This is because managerialism neglects particular aspects of public service, such as fairness, participation and professional motivation of staff to improve services and respond to public needs.

Another feature of managerialism is to delegate decision-making to the local level, leaving managers 'free to manage'. An example is care management in the community care reforms. However, this policy is carried out in an overall philosophy of increasingly centralised control needed to pursue corporate objectives through 'joined-up policy'.

These factors suggest, then, that the claims of managerialism to be able to reform how public servants do their job are inconsistent with important aspects of public service. They are also internally inconsistent in seeking *both* devolution of responsibility *and* centralised control.

Impractical and unrealistic
Managerialism assumes that private sector management techniques are appropriate to the public sector, without looking at the detailed differences between the two settings. First, public servants are accountable to elected representatives who make decisions to achieve political rather than efficiency-seeking objectives. The private sector can measure success by profit, but the public service has multiple, conflicting goals and priorities. Private sector organisations generally have competitors, but public service organisations rarely have competing organisations. In private sector organisations, supply is related to income: the more services or goods a manager supplies, the more the organisation's income grows. It is exactly the opposite in the public sector. There, the more the manager supplies, the greater the cost, and in the public sector, costs are constrained by the capacity or preparedness of the public to pay taxes. Charges are only weakly related to costs, and when politicians make in-principle decisions to ration some service, they often cannot maintain the decision when it receives media attention. For all these reasons, the structure of public services prevents managers from being price-responsive.

In the private sector, consumers are regarded as a bundle of desires which can be stimulated by advertising and then satisfied. This has some application in the public service, and 'customer-care' policies have led to improvements in public services. However, the consumer in public services, for example, a disabled person seeking provision of aids and adaptations, is a citizen with rights. Moreover those rights are often achieved and enforced by collective, political action rather than payment of charges to a provider which is free to provide as much as is desired. Rather, the public service is there to ration and control provision. Also, many public services, such as child protection, are compulsory or regulatory and supplied against the will of the client. Therefore, some essential bases on which private sector managerialism relies are absent or irrelevant in the public sector.

Staff management
Managerialism fails to recognise that staff in the public services are in a significantly different position from those in the private sector. There are generally considerable constraints on the authority of line managers to hire, fire and promote. This means that the 'freedom to manage' requirement of managerialism is not present. Also, there are national payscales and awards which are restricted by the political need for limiting public sector expenditure. This means that sums of money which might realistically be motivating cannot be offered as incentives, except to a very few. In reality, then, financial incentives are limited to the few most senior managers at the top of organisations so division and resentment result.

Another factor is that there are many groups of workers in the public sector who have professional allegiances. Sometimes this offers opportunities to resist requirements to comply with managerial demands on ethical or professional grounds. There are some such professionals in the private sector (for example, engineers, architects, accountants). However, in the private sector ethical behaviour is often effective for the employer. An example is that civil engineers building bridges must behave ethically, otherwise bridges might collapse. Thus, ethical behaviour is necessary for both the employer and the professional. Alternatively, private sector professionals have limited roles bound by outside controls (for example, accountants as auditors). If these controls do not work, professionals' roles in the private sector are sometimes twisted by employers' requirements (for example, the architect who cuts corners on house-building, creative accounting). In the public sector, professionals are also bound by significant and complex legal requirements which are a limitation on the 'right to manage'. They impose other requirements such as 'fairness' by procedures such as judicial review.

Political critique

This aspect of the critique of managerialism examines which groups derive material and political benefits from the dominance of this approach. These are generally management consultants and accountancy firms which specialise in measurement and quantification. Other gainers include companies which obtain financial benefits from privatisation and marketisation. Also, some senior managers gain by achieving 'right to manage' jobs outside the public sector payscales, and increase their income as a result. Disadvantaged groups, on the other hand, include low-paid public sector workers whose jobs were privatised and who suffered therefore greater insecurity and loss of income and job-related benefits. There have also been effects on public sector managers who can see advantages for themselves of becoming managers rather than low-paid public sector professionals. Similarly, public sector consumers can see advantages for themselves in becoming, say, owners rather than renters of housing or having rights over and income from, fostered children rather than providing a public service. These changes from managerialism change the political debate and assumptions that workers and service users make about the nature and value of the services they deal with.

Value critique

Managerialism supports values of efficiency, economy and effectiveness rather than values of fairness, justice, participation and rights to representation. This is because the underlying political and economic philosophy is individualism, in which it is considered desirable to encourage individuals to be free to pursue their own interests as much as possible. However, this mainly benefits managers and people with money to win in the market. It does not benefit clients without resources or, of course, workers who must be controlled. If they are allowed to do so freely, managerialist views argue, a market will develop which accords people their wishes. Public sector philosophies of collectivism focus on the need for sharing responsibility and rights together with mutual protection.

The shift to managerialism, particularly of the political and economic kind, has partly come about because of some of the problems discussed in Chapter 1. That is, worry about having too much bureaucracy in state services has led people to say that the state is not a good, flexible manager of services to the public. Over-bureaucratic state services offer fertiliser for a gardener to bring on the plants of marketisation and privatisation which the average member of the public might regard as weeds if public services met needs better. This makes the connection to consumerism too.

Consumerism, managerialism and social work

How is consumerism related to managerialism and economic rationalism? Many people see it as something entirely different, so here I want to spell out the connection. It is the idea of choice in a market. Economic rationalism focuses on giving people choice in a market as a response to problems of state management. Consumerism is based on facilitating effective choice for people receiving goods and services. That is why the two ideas are connected. For people to have choice, they need access to services, information about the possibilities and what they might be entitled to. Sometimes they also need representation to argue for their rights (Potter, 1988).

Crucially, consumerism assumes that people have power to walk away from a service or that various alternatives are available among which they can freely choose. An example of proposals for social work services that rely on consumerism is the Wagner report on residential care (1988). It argues that residential care should be a 'positive choice' for potential residents. To make this work, the Report proposes that residential care must be seen as part of a range of services, with people being able to make choices among the alternatives. Of course, everyone has such power to some extent, but most of the social services do not work like this. In child protection, court orders may require or press parents to comply with supervision. The children have rights to be consulted, more so as they grow older, but decisions are frequently made for them. In community care, the whole basis of the system is in making plans involving the user, but controlled by the resources available to commissioning services. There is very little effective choice at all.

Moreover, as Powell (1991) argues, defining people as 'service users' or 'consumers' represents them as being in a relationship with the social worker similar to the relationship of a customer or consumer in a commercial market. They are claimed to be able to seek a service and treated as being able to make a choice of what is to be provided to them. However, this is not the reality of the situation. 'Service users' are not in the same relationship as a customer because they do not pay and have the ultimate control of being able to choose something else. If they do not accept the service, they are usually choosing to have nothing. The worker is making the choices, or constraining the available alternatives, based on resource constraints or political decisions about what will be available. In addition, many social work clients are compelled to receive social work services. Examples are where mentally ill people are compulsorily admitted to mental hospitals or offenders and abusive parents are required to accept supervision.

To marry these positions up to one which claims a customer relationship, the user is entitled to an 'assessment' or be dealt with appropriately in a process. So, in child care, children have rights to have their 'wishes and feelings' considered in decision-making, but the decisions are made in their 'best interests'. Similarly, administrative discretion limits many 'users' rights. In community care, for example, the right to have 'needs' assessed is negated in the published government guidance by reserving the right to define need to the agency (Payne, 1995, pp75–6). Parents of children looked after by the local authority, who may be affected by official decisions, have few rights and powers to protect their own position. To defend or gain public acceptance of the decisions, the major factor is how well the process of assessment and decision-making takes place. Thus, what information is gathered, who has been consulted, and how the decision is made, become more important than the content of the decision. This is why procedure becomes so important that it undermines, as Powell argues, the use of discretion and judgement conventionally required of professionals. It leads to what Middleton (1994) calls a 'tyranny of procedure'. Anti-bureaucratic social work implies moving back to the content of the decision and away from this focus on quality in a process. Social work is about the impact of the outcomes on people, as well as the quality of the processes they experience.

However, outcomes cannot be pursued separately from users' experiences of process. One example is national performance indicators for social services which the government proposes to introduce (DoH, 1999). These specify proportions of particular outcomes of service that SSDs should try to attain, for example that a low proportion of children being looked after should be moved during each year. The advantages of doing so are consistency of provision and an approximation of responding to people's needs, by treating generally-defined purposes as appropriate for all. The problem is that the proper cautions about flexibility, contained in the consultation document, are often translated into crude compliance requirements. In the 'do-not-move-looked-after-children' example, managers will not know the proportion moved already in the year or the proportion likely to be moved later in the year. Therefore, there will be a tendency to prohibit any movement. This might be reasonable and fit with what the research says would be desirable. In particular cases, however, dealing flexibly with a child who needs to be moved could well be obstructed by bureaucratic requirements designed to keep the proportion of movements down. Such approaches treat social services which must deal with complex human situations services as though they are capable of technical planning, like bridge-building.

Pfeffer and Coote (1991) argue that approaches to quality assurance like these are inappropriately drawn from commercial activities. They suggest that public services need to offer equity and participation. Users can be helped to make their own definitions of needs and the ways in which they might be met. Services organised according to principles imposed from the top down may fit with policy-makers' conceptions of what they want to achieve. However, this approach is inconsistent with what social work is about. This is so when the requirements are for social work services and require compliance from social workers. It may also be so for other services where social workers have to argue for flexibility elsewhere on behalf of their clients. As we saw above, it also reveals an inconsistency within the heart of the managerialist ideas. That is centralised control, and policy-making does not fit well with devolving power and decision-making so that it might be more responsive to users' wishes. Hadley and Clough (1996, p 196), in their survey of workers' experience of community care services after the reforms introduced in the early 1990s, suggest that the complex interpersonal relationship between client and social worker is quite unlike the simple customer-salesperson relationship of the market.

Evidence for this comes from two surveys during the 1990s of 'whistleblowing' in the social services (Hunt and Campbell, 1998). These extensive surveys found that social workers were aware of frequent lapses of good practice. Investigation of their experience suggests that managers were less interested in the practice of workers with their clients than in achieving corporate objectives. As a result, instances of poor practice, while well-known, went unchecked because these did not matter in achieving the managers' set objectives. In this way, the service's management objectives were achieved, but these did not focus on users' experiences of good quality professional practice.

To sum up this part of the argument, I have suggested that trying to achieve good practice through procedures will not work, because the outcomes for users must be an important factor in quality practice. However, focusing entirely on outcomes ignores the importance of users' experiences of quality practice as they are dealt with in a service which mainly deals with individuals' complex human problems. Therefore, to enhance quality practice management must deal both with process and outcome, but it cannot operate through procedures. Once procedures have been followed, there is often still a remaining need for flexibility and humanity required in social work. It must also include a judgement about the human and social impact of the outcomes of service provision. Service users' views of their experience must also be a factor. However, this is not the purpose of consumerism based on the commercial market, which assumes a simpler relationship between the service provider's input and the consumer's satisfaction.

So pursuing consumerism is in many ways inconsistent with the requirements of managing the social services, indeed many other public services too. Using managerialist approaches in public services further divorces them from the requirements of equity and participation for the client and flexibility and judgement by the worker. Performance indicators and procedural approaches to managing services attempt to maintain the quality of services in the absence of that sense of equity, involvement, flexibility and judgement. Procedural equality, that is treating people by the same processes, is only a weak proxy for substantive equality (Weale, 1978), that is achieving a good outcome which reflects what the different individuals need and want. Substantive equality is a more appropriate aim for social work than procedural equality. It allows services to respond to what individuals want and need rather than what policy assumes the generality of people want and need.

Relevance to social work
Managerialism and its political environment have a particular relevance to social work, and it is easy to see why this is so when we look at the features of managerialism and the critique of it which I reviewed above.

Social work is one of those local government professions whose loyalty is to values defined outside the management requirements of government policy. Its work is bounded by and constructed from legal responsibilities. This contrasts with, say, youth and community work, whose existence in any area and the way it is provided is largely discretionary. Social work is a relatively low-paid public service profession, significantly concerned with social control and regulating people's lives, as in child protection, or in rationing services, as in community care. Therefore, consumer choice and generous work-related benefits to motivate employers are not a realistic possibility. Social work is thus the epitome of bureau-professionalism which the new Right sought to challenge through, among other things, managerialism. It was an essential part of the flexibility in the bureaucratic system.

Social work, then, is one of those professions which will not be very susceptible to managerialist control. On the other hand, as part of a system of bureau-professionalism, social work has several features which indicate that it is likely to lean towards bureaucracy rather than flexible professionalism. Unlike medicine or law, it does not have a tradition of independent practitioners operating outside organisational control. It was late in professionalisation; many field social workers were not trained until the 1970s. Compared with related professions, it has a relatively short period of training in Britain. It also has a long history within local government and, further back, within the Poor Law. Consequently, people see it appropriately as an administrative provision within the normal bounds of local government rather than a profession requiring expertise. Moreover, the subject matter of social work offers a weak knowledge base. Many people do not accept its value as the basis for action or for a profession: more 'scientific' professions have a more influential knowledge base. Also, it works in arenas where many people who are not social workers have experiences which they regard as valid social work knowledge to form the basis for action. Sometimes they think their experiences are more valid than social work knowledge.

These factors mean that people do not accept its independence, and managers and politicians judge that non-expert management is perfectly possible. To the outsider who has not looked carefully or thought about what might be involved, there is nothing really specialised to know. The obvious possibility, therefore, is to control social work through bureaucratic regulation and procedure. Discretionary knowledge, it might be argued, will not get in the way, and lack of specialised knowledge means that detailed specification of the work should be possible for a competent management system.

Social work, managerialism and bureaucracy
The impact of managerialism has affected social work, therefore, in ways special to its social position. Its weakness as a profession means that it cannot resist managerialism by claiming distinctive knowledge, skills and values or powerful rights to professional discretion: this is everywhere contested. However, the weaknesses of managerialism, faced with an occupation that

requires a good deal of discretion and professional judgement to work at all, have led to a reassertion of bureaucratic inflexibility. This is a way of appearing to manage according to managerialist corporate policy which has grown out of 'economic rationalism'. Moreover, social work is largely provided within local government which took the brunt of the new Right managerialist policy to control expenditure through redefining the political and economic 'settlement'.

We can add the commentary contained in Chapter 1 to these points. There we saw that the British political system, backed up by social pressures, is particularly susceptible to centralised political control and secrecy. That susceptibility is supported by legal and organisational requirements which lead to the use of bureaucratic organisation and authority. Managerialism backs our centralised, authoritarian system with further pressure for control, using methods and following management ideologies which are inimical to flexibility. Implement this in a weak profession, unable to protect itself through individual practice backed by accepted and well-developed knowledge, skills and values and it is a recipe for bureaucratic inflexibility.

Another important issue is the fact that many users of social services are 'excluded' groups who are stigmatised by the public in general. Because they are marginal to powerful decision-makers such as industrialists and planners, users of social services, among them sick, unemployed and poor people, are not going to achieve an impact as consumers. Instead they are going to be regarded as the objects of policy, not the subjects of initiatives to help them gain control and influence over the social environment of their own lives. Moreover the social control and regulatory aspect of social work means that some 'clients' of social work are not 'users' of service. They are more like the 'customers' of the local police station. This means that they are stigmatised, their illegal or disapproved activities or personas are likely to lead to further exclusion. 'Why should we help *those* people?' 'Why should we bother with people who do that?' These are common questions asked about the people social workers work with. I once worked in a local authority where the chief executive would point out that social services clients were nearly all people who did not pay taxes.

These attitudes inevitably rub off on social workers and the social services. Since they work with '*those* people', they are inevitably going to be associated with support for them. As a result, the profession is stigmatised just as strongly as the clients they work with.

Social work – unloved and unwanted?
Sometimes this feeling that social work is an unloved profession because of the people it works with is exaggerated. For one thing, many people have some contact with social services agencies. Middle-aged people often have contact about elderly relatives. A high proportion of people have some involvement with mental health services. Foster carers and adopters also become involved with social services. People using hospitals will often receive social work in a supportive or counselling mode. Disabled people come from all walks of life. So not everyone who uses social work services comes from stigmatised groups. Not everyone is subjected to the kind of social work which exercises social control over their lives. Many people must go away with a positive understanding of the role of social work in society. Indeed, consumer studies suggest that many clients have quite a positive view of the help they get from social workers.

How may we interpret the feeling that social work is disapproved of and disliked? One way is to view the new Right managerialist project as inherently hostile to the purposes and character of social work. We have noted above that much of the critique of managerialism suggests that it fails to take into account many important features of public services, and has been applied inappropriately. However, in many instances, even at its height, Thatcherism did not seek to get rid of social work. Instead, its legislation (the Children Act, 1989, and the NHS and Community Care Act, 1990) strengthened social work and gave it more responsibilities. After the Barclay report of 1982 justified social work's tasks and roles, the social work role has been largely preserved. However, its function has been diverted to the managerialist purpose of control rather than its helping and therapeutic purposes. Another interpretation relies on the influence of the media which is fundamentally conservative in its ownership and in the policies it espouses. Therefore, it is likely to be hostile to the more open and flexible elements of social work. The answer might be to accept that there will always be an element of criticism towards more flexible and open supportive approaches in British culture. We can see this in the impression that social work is much more accepted and acceptable in Nordic cultures, which are more socialist in their cultural assumptions.

However, these justifications seem a little too easy. Also, they ignore the argument of Clarke and Newman (1997), discussed above, about the breakdown in the 'settlement' in which bureau-professions like social work were established and became influential. The bureaucratic element has broken down because political acceptance of the 'rules' has withered away in the face of greater diversity. The imposition of new Right policies through managerialism is also challenged. On the other hand, the political–economic settlement has also broken down, so the expectation of service provision as a right to citizens has also been lost. As part of the battleground for the achievement of a new settlement, or for retaining elements of the old, social work's role has become less agreed and less acceptable. Moreover, managerialism claims, misleadingly, that effectiveness of consumer choice will be provided through public services, when all that can be provided is procedural equality within a rationing process.

If we then turn to the social order roles of social work, similar difficulties arise. The old settlement placed social work as a profession which supported an agreed social order. Thus, parenting behaviour would be adjusted to conventionally acceptable approaches; delinquency would be controlled, mental illness and all kinds of disabilities would be hidden and managed. All this would assure people of their safety and security in an established order. But that order is no longer established. The economic settlement no longer permits extensive institutionalisation of disabled and mentally ill people. The broader acceptance of diversity requires inclusion rather than exclusion of many groups of people. Yet some people feel insecure much of the time, and all people feel insecure some of the time. This happens because we have not yet learned how to manage and support that diversity and integrate it within a more complex society. So, with people with learning disabilities or mental illnesses, we swing from being controlling and restrictive to trying to open up provision. In parenting, sometimes we want to accept a range of different ethnic and class assumptions about parenting, and a range of sexuality and family structures. At others, we want some of that range restricted to conform with our own values, forgetting that our own values differ from those of others within the range.

In sum, then, social work is caught up in a battle to achieve a new settlement within society. It is criticised by the new social movements because it cannot deliver the kind of society that recognises and responds to diversity and flexibility. At the same time it is criticised by the new Right for failing to provide the safety and security of the old settlement. Many people talk, perhaps from ignorance, about social work's lack of realism and the failure to control some clients. They complain of too much of a focus on doing good, and not enough on ensuring that others behave well. That is a sign of the breakdown of the national patriarchal social settlement. At the same time, people say that the services they want are not provided and social work is inflexible and bureaucratic. That is a sign of the breakdown of the political–economic settlement of welfare for all. The diversity, flexibility and high expenditure required is not recognised by the traditional patriarchal, full-male-employment settlement.

A new kind of social work required
If the old settlement has broken down, a new kind of social work is required. The question is: what would it look like? The managerialist agenda proposes a constrained, managed, planned, scientific social work, in the managerialist image. It would use task-centred practice so that there are clear objectives. It would use cognitive-behavioural theories because they have been proven to work. What we have found in the Chapter, though, is that this approach is a politically motivated mirage. It is one unrealistic side of the broken-down settlements we are trying to replace.

However, the wish to return to a bureau-professional style of work is also untenable. The diversity of modern British society makes it impossible. Professional judgement exercised in an authoritarian, patriarchal bureaucracy is unacceptable to a culture in which many diverse political and social relationships must be acknowledged.

Somehow, social work has to achieve a new balance between the need for security and certainty and the culture of diversity and openness. That is what anti-bureaucratic social work offers. I propose that it contains two main elements, represented in the next two chapters. First, it contains an explicit commitment to representing the diversity, giving it a voice and investing that voice with power and influence. An important way of doing so is by promoting advocacy within the professional role and providing advocacy services under the control of service users. The second element, represented in Chapter 4, is an approach to social work which breaks down the influence of authoritarian, patriarchal bureaucratic behaviour. We should replace it with an openness. That openness must be managed to offer certainty in the nature, style and outcomes of service provision and security and safety in the contribution it makes to society. Does that mean that social work does not or cannot contribute to change because it must offer that element of social order in its role? I argue not, because the new social order requires constant change in response to diverse and changing cultures in our society. That is the focus of Chapter 5.

Chapter 3
ADVOCACY

Introduction: why advocacy in anti-bureaucratic social work?

What are we going to do about the ill-effects of bureaucratic inflexibility and managerialism in social work and the social services? One answer to this question is: 'advocacy'. It is a well-established social work skill and ethical responsibility to act on behalf of our clients within our own organisation and with other organisations. Moreover, recently, the demand for effective consumer involvement in services has emphasised the value of advocacy on behalf of service users. Clienthood is assumed to mean that they will be incapable of speaking for themselves. This even comes from some managerialist ideas about consumerism, although as we have seen, partly perverted by the influence of managerialism in the public sector. One consequence of this perversion is that social workers feel that they cannot advocate for their clients because they have power over them and must impose the local authority's policies. This managerialist emphasis on the authority of the agency confuses different meanings and purposes of advocacy.

In this Chapter, I want to look at advocacy both as an aspect of social work and as a service for and involving service users. However, I also argue that it is not enough of an answer to the 'what are we going to do . . . ?' question. We need a specific focus on anti-bureaucratic practice. I take that up in the next Chapter.

There is a very positive view of advocacy at present in the social services and yet a curious caution about it. Some colleagues and I carried out a research project to investigate the introduction of an advocacy service for mentally ill people in a particular area (Emerson, *et al.*, 1994). The response from the professionals involved was pretty much universal – they all thought it was a desirable development. The argument was that it should be independent of the existing services. Then, it could genuinely speak up for mentally ill people, without ties to the organisations which provided services. It would give confidence to the mentally ill people, both in the community and in hospital, that they could have an independent and influential voice on their side.

As part of the research, I asked people whether they thought that they, as professionals, had an advocacy role. Nurses accepted this: it is written into their Code of Professional Conduct. They were sure that advocacy was an essential part of what they did. The Commentary on the Code says:

*'The introductory paragraphs of the Code of Professional Conduct . . .
indicate clearly the expectation that the practitioner will accept a role as
advocate on behalf of his or her patients/clients. Some tend to want to
identify advocacy as a separate and distinct subject. It is not. It is a
component of many professional activities of this and other professions. . .*

*. . . **Advocacy is concerned with promoting and safeguarding the
wellbeing and interests of patients and clients. It is not concerned with
conflict for its own sake.** It is important that this fact is recognised, since
some practitioners seem to regard advocacy on behalf of patients or
clients as an adversarial activity and feel either attracted to it or not able
to accept it for that reason . . .*

*. . . **The Code of Professional Conduct envisages the role of patient or
client advocate as an integral and essential aspect of good professional
practice.'***   [Source: UKCC (1984) pp 12–13, emphasis original)

I think imposing this sort of professional requirement can be influential, provided
the managers see themselves as professionals pursuing a professional agenda.
Managerialism prevents this; its commitment to 'joined-up policy' rejects professional discretion. In this way, managerialism works against consumer interests as
interpreted by professionals. If it does so, where does it get its views of the
consumer interest from? The managerialist view would be that we should get the
consumer view directly, by surveys, complaints systems and quality assurance
processes. Again, we see here an inadequacy of the managerialist philosophy. In
public services, the job is at least partly social control and rationing, not, as in a
shop, offering as much as possible to whoever seeks it. This leads to significant
social divisions between consumers and workers in the public service. Such
social divisions are added to the professional division, where workers are 'expert'
helpers; they are 'subjects', able to act of their own accord. Users, on the other
hand are 'objects': people who are acted upon by others, 'unknowing' or
'dependent' receivers of help. People receiving public services are often
excluded from political and decision-making processes. They may have a vote,
but the pressures of their lives give them more things to think about than influencing the political agenda on their own behalf. The mere fact that they have
problems reduces their credibility in political and social influence.

The powers, roles and responsibilities of the social services, then, mean that we
must find ways of representing the needs of its service users in ways other than
the conventional consumerist approach. Political influence is often ineffective
for them too. Therefore, strengthening their voice in decision-making about
their own affairs and, more broadly, in planning and policy-making is a vital
part of an anti-bureaucratic service. One important way of doing this is through
advocacy provision.

Types of advocacy

It is customary to distinguish two types of advocacy. One, *case advocacy*, is where the advocate argues on behalf of someone. This is the meaning attached to advocacy by lawyers who act on behalf of their clients in court. The other form, *cause advocacy*, is where the advocate argues for a change in belief, attitude, policy or organisation which would benefit a category of people. These two classic forms of advocacy are related. Pressure groups have always used an accumulation of cases, which individually would be case advocacy, to argue for a change in policy, which would be cause advocacy. Achieving a change in policy through cause advocacy would inevitably benefit and remove difficulties in many individual cases.

During the 1970s and very strongly in the 1980s, however, an advocacy movement grew up. It focused on providing advocacy for stigmatised and oppressed people who were often clients of social workers. There are several different types, as follows (Brandon *et al.*, 1995):

- *Citizen advocacy* grew up in the field of learning disability. This was because people with learning disabilities were identified as not having the intellectual ability to argue for themselves in very complex services dominated by strong professions. Citizen advocacy services recruited volunteers to get to know people with learning difficulties over a period of time and to act for them in all sorts of official processes. The problem with this arrangement is that it may be hard for the person with learning disabilities to distinguish between the citizen advocate and the myriad of other helpers who seek to make relationships with them. It may also be hard for the volunteer to maintain the boundaries between being an advocate and being a counsellor or helper in a broader way.

- *Self-advocacy* was a response to some of the difficulties of citizen advocacy. The approach is to train and support people with learning disabilities to act on their own behalf. However, while desirable from the point of view of stimulating independence, this could put increasing pressure on individuals.

- *Group advocacy* developed to support individual self-advocates. Groups of service users would be established. The group would take responsibility alongside individuals for advocating in particular situations where they could not do this for themselves. Members of the group would help each other in this way. Also, the group formed a support while the individual was pursuing self-advocacy.

- *Peer advocacy* developed from self-help organisations, particularly for people with disabilities or who are recovering from mental illnesses. Peer advocacy provides a basis for self- and group advocacy which relies on people who share similar experiences. Some members would have recovered or developed their situation so that they were not under so much pressure individually as a group of self-advocates might be.

- *Professional advocacy* is an aspect of provision which has grown up particularly in services for children and young people. Here, children clearly need to have their voices heard, but are often inexperienced in dealing with adult mechanisms for discussion and decision. Therefore, arranging for professional support in expressing their views, both by their social workers or keyworkers or by independent services is an important area of development (Dalrymple and Hough, 1995).

These approaches extended the understanding of advocacy, and created an environment in which advocacy became an important aspect of provision in many areas. Service-user groups mainly organised advocacy services themselves. Unfortunately, these developments also de-emphasised the role of advocacy by social workers and other professionals on behalf of their clients. This led to the situation where social workers felt it was inappropriate or impossible for them to pursue advocacy on behalf of their clients. They felt it should only be done by advocacy organisations involving users themselves. The development of managerialist approaches to social services management also affected them. Managerialism de-emphasises responsibility for service users and the role of being on the side of service users, and over-emphasises compliance with management perspectives and the responsibility for resource control. This then places the balance against this outside the professional – with a representative advocacy service. The managers can then insist on compliance from their workers.

However, though social workers have those responsibilities, they also have responsibilities for acting on behalf of their clients: the word 'client' emphasises that point. A lawyer's, architect's or accountant's client has the right to instruct them what to do. Where judgements have to be made, the professional may be given freedom to act, within limits specified by the client. Alternatively, they may have to explain what they intend to do and get approval from the client. Ethical requirements also limit the range of instructions that a client can give. An architect cannot be required to build a house that does not comply with the building regulations or with the engineering requirements of safety. It is the same with social workers. Clients, in the conventional meaning of the term, give them general guidance about what they want, but expect workers to use their skills appropriately and refer back to them if necessary. We saw in Chapter 2 that managerialism de-emphasises this kind of client control in favour of an unrealistic user or customer perspective.

Advocacy in social work

Advocacy has a long history within social work. It has always been regarded as a skill that social workers should have. Long ago, Attlee (1920), the only social work academic to become prime minister, argued that social workers should be 'agitators' on behalf of their clients. Barbara Wootton (1959), attacked excessively therapeutic social work, arguing that social workers should mainly act on behalf of their clients in dealing with the complexities of the modern welfare state. Analyses of social work skills, first done comprehensively in the 1970s, always came out with advocacy as a crucial skill and function of social workers (Payne, 1982, ch. 4). Advocacy has also always been an essential aspect of professional codes of ethics in social work.

For example, the British Code (BASW, 1996, para 9) says:

> *'The social worker's responsibility for relief and prevention of hardship and suffering is not always fully discharged by direct service to individual families and groups. The worker has the right and duty to bring to the attention of those in power, and of the general public, ways in which the activities of government, society or agencies, create or contribute to hardship and suffering or militate against their relief. Social workers are often at the interface between powerful organisations and relatively powerless applicants for service. While social workers are accountable to those under whose authority they work, and responsible for the efficient performance of their task and for their management of the organisations' resources, these must be balanced against their professional responsibility to their client...'*

So, why was advocacy neglected? One important reason is found in this ethical statement: 'the duty to provide advocacy is a balance between the authority of the organisation and the professional duty'. We have seen above and in previous chapters that managerialism over-emphasises the organisation against the ethical duty. The balance must be restored.

However, there were also failings within social work. One problem was the focus until the 1970s on interpersonal work with clients as the main role of social workers. Social work writers and social work training examined this in great detail. The indirect roles of social work, where social workers acted on behalf of clients with others, were neglected. Mobilising resources, liaison and other similar roles were as neglected as advocacy. They were taken for granted as things that any educated adult could do. Changes in social work theory brought these aspects of social work back into focus. Systems theory, which became influential in the mid-1970s, re-emphasised that the 'target system' with which social workers intervened might easily not be the client or the client's family. It might be another agency or elsewhere in society. Viewing work with other agencies as an important part of social work threw the spotlight on case advocacy, whereas previously, psychological therapeutic theories had concentrated on changing clients' behaviour. Radical theory, also influential in the early 1970s, argued that an essential aspect of social work was changing the policy and practices of social structures so that the needs and rights of oppressed and excluded people were met. This reaffirmed cause advocacy as a role of social work. One important method of radical work was a concern for welfare rights, that is, advocacy in the social security system.

Consequently, the 1970s saw a flowering of case and, to some extent, cause advocacy within the social security system. Welfare rights services have grown up, becoming important services both separately and as a part of social work. This became particularly important as new Right policies to constrain the costs of the welfare state began to bite in the 1980s. Skill development improved (eg Bateman, 1995) and the idea of 'principled advocacy' grew up. This means trying to get as much for clients as possible, without colluding with the oppressive aspects of the system.

Radical social work also emphasised the importance of social workers being on the side of their clients, even within an oppressive social services system. In the USA, the Ad Hoc Committee on Advocacy (1969) was an influential group emphasising the advocacy role of social workers, particularly in cause advocacy. At much the same time, the development of systems theory and work on defining the skills involved in generic social work emphasised both therapeutic interpersonal skills, and indirect skills of practice. Examples were liaison, negotiating, mobilising resources and, among them, advocacy. Many of these skills are used in advocacy, since advocacy is not straight arguing or presenting a case involving presentation skills. It involves preparing the way for a client, arranging a deal for them with another agency, organising resources that they can use.

From the 1970s onwards, another factor grew in importance: the role of social work as the gatekeeper of the entry point to a range of services. Domiciliary services blossomed after SSDs were set up and probation services developed a range of interventions within day and residential care provision. Such develop-ments in provision meant that social workers had more to offer than simply their own interpersonal work. Receiving clients' applications or requests for services, converting them into waiting list places and arguing for resources to be used for clients became an increasingly crucial part of social workers' roles.

Rationing vs. advocacy

Should we see this as rationing or advocacy? It is a bit of both. It is the agency which rations, using the social worker's arguments and information to decide. This is made clear in the care management role which many social workers took up after the community care reforms of the early 1990s (Payne, 1995). Here, the care manager, often a social worker, finds out the information and has the role of putting together a package of services for the client. Policy is that the worker should involve the client and carers in deciding the package. However, the process is controlled by a budget that is usually inadequate. One policy purpose of the reforms was to make workers more aware of and responsive to budgetary issues. What consequences does this have for the advocacy element of the social worker's role? Inevitably, concern for the budget constrains workers' concerns for clients' wishes. Moreover, they are put in a negotiating position with users and carers, so they appear to be on the side of rationing against users' wishes. Users and carers cannot be certain that the worker is negotiating to change their minds for good professional reasons or for budgetary reasons.

The dual advocacy/rationing role therefore presents problems for social workers, since their organisation and its managers must ration, and they are subject to the power and influence of their managers. When social workers make the case for clients, they inevitably have to consider their position in long-standing relationships with their superiors. If they fight too assertively this time, they may have more difficulty next time. Also, they are party to the decisions, so they cannot be fully on the client's side; at some point they accede to negotiating pressures. This may also lead to dishonesty in the relationship with the user. An example of dishonesty might be where workers feel that they have to present the department's proposals positively. One reason for doing so is that these might be the best available and users might be discouraged from taking what they can get. Another example is where the worker presents the outcome as a good one, or the best that could be achieved, when they have compromised in the negotiation for all sorts of organisational reasons.

The possibility of this sort of dishonesty happening leads people to argue for all advocacy to be undertaken by independent organisations, whose role is to be solely on the side of clients. However, this is a naive proposal. For one thing, look at other professions. Lawyers, in spite of their role to argue their client's position, do not do so with the full force of their skill on every occasion. Lawyers know when a position is credible to a court, or when the police will not accept an argument for bail, and temper their approach accordingly. The doctor might claim to make decisions wholly to the benefit of patients, but doctors make resource decisions about who should get operations or expensive medication. This was made explicit with general practitioner fundholding in the early 1990s. It continues in the new primary care groups commissioning local services developed by the new Labour government in the later 1990s. Doctors decide where people go on waiting lists. Social workers, then, are in no radically different position from other professionals who negotiate and ration as part of their professional judgements.

Secondly, social workers form the operational arm of the decision-making process which actually meets users and carers to identify and assess their needs. It is inevitable that they are going to have an influence on resource decision-making, whether or not the user also has an advocate immovably committed to their instructions. The face-to-face communication that workers experience can have a high impact on a decision. This is because so much of the other input to decision-making is less vivid being statistical, procedural or paper-based. So social workers' advocacy for users' needs is going to continue to be powerful, even though they and the users may perceive it differently. What I think is necessary here is not to deny the advocacy role and the role of professional decision-making and judgement.

Within this framework, social workers need to maintain the idea of clients getting a fair hearing and having their rights met. They are entitled to proper consideration for their needs and, by specific policy decision, involvement in the process of decision-making. Therefore, many decision-making processes in social work agencies require careful and complete representation of clients' views. The requirement for anti-bureaucratic social work is that the agency also recognises within its processes that social workers have the role to provide an aspect of that representation. Otherwise, their responsibilities for client involvement are not being properly accepted. However, it is important that social workers are open in holding this balance. Otherwise, they become entangled in the tyranny of procedure, identified in Chapter 2. Also, they might fail to meet their ethical responsibilities, outlined in the Code of Ethics, discussed above.

This balance is much clearer in social workers' regulatory roles, where they try to manage offenders' behaviour. Other examples are the consequences of mentally ill people's problems or where they decide on child abuse or adoption cases. In many situations, social workers make decisions that are sometimes tough and which frequently compel clients to do things that they do not want. However, this does not negate trying to do the best for the welfare and progress of the client and others involved such as carers, adoptive parents and foster carers. The social work role involves pushing forward what clients and others need and want, within the legal and professional limits, and recognising the different and sometimes conflicting interests of those involved. The limitations of managerialism prevent social workers from using the flexibility that this complex range of conflicting opportunities and priorities requires. Elderly users of community care services are just as aware as social workers of the conflicts between their interests and needs and those of their informal carers. It is therefore legitimate and wise to raise and resolve such conflicts of interest openly but this needs skill. Just because a client is forced to accept the agency's decisions in some respects, it should not prevent the worker from helping them to be independent in other aspects of their lives. Just because a client has to accept the less-than-ideal because funding is insufficient, it should not prevent the worker from making sure that their interests are properly represented in the decision-making process.

Community work and social action
Other forms of social work using social work skills have a close relationship with advocacy for individual clients. Many social workers take part in community work as an aspect of their roles: they help support self-help groups, mutual aid, local community groups and voluntary sector services. Sometimes, community work and social action pursues social work purposes, through seeking local-level or policy-level social change.

Doing this kind of social work means acting on behalf of clients and users in a different kind of way. More often it involves acting alongside and with them rather than as a professional who does things for them. It involves promoting natural resources which help clients, rather than welfare services which stand outside the mainstream of community experience. Clearly, then, this involves advocating on behalf of clients' and users' needs, because the worker is taking up those needs and helping to have them met through clients' own community resources.

Promoting and developing such activities through service development and commissioning work, through locality commissioning and such processes, agencies can accept some of the responsibility of this aspect of representing clients' needs as well.

Engaging with the agency
We have seen that advocacy is not just an interpersonal matter, getting things done for clients, or getting them the service they are entitled to or wish for. It may

involve wider work on the client's cause. If social workers are doing that as part of their ordinary work, as opposed to operating in an advocacy service, they will be doing it with both other agencies and their own. It may be easier to feel confident about trying to get another agency to change their approach. Our own agency may support us in that. However, many social workers feel it is impossible to seek to change their own agency. This is going beyond what we have discussed, simply arguing for clients' and users' needs in their own agency. We are talking here about changing the agency in its response to the needs not only of specific users', but all users in general. Are social workers not required to comply with what their agency wants in both cases? We have seen in the previous argument that, ethically, they take on a dual role and must find a balance in arguing for users' and clients' needs. However, we have also seen that this is commonplace in other professions. Most professions have to hold a balance between user, agency and their own professional judgement. Managerialism means that agencies will press for the resolution in their own favour. The role often involves clients' rights within the agency to a fair hearing and proper presentation of their case and their wishes. Whatever the brutality or foot-dragging of its management, it is hard for a public organisation to argue against that.

Being a good advocate as a social worker means understanding such circumstances and how to act in them. Advocating for individuals or even for social and policy change to respond to the causes that individuals' problems raise, is insufficient within the social services. Adequate advocacy within social services requires engagement with the organisation providing the service. The organisation must be at least prepared to consider change to allow advocacy to become effective. Beyond that, to work for the user also requires that the organisation change. In the next few paragraphs, I recount some experiences which have led me to believe this.

In one of the research projects that I have undertaken on advocacy, I followed the work of advocates in a major child care agency over seventeen months. Like most such schemes, the advocate helped the young person formulate a complaint. This was then taken on and investigated by a designated complaints officer in the organisation, the child being represented throughout the process by the advocate. The scheme was stymied by one bugbear. At an informal level, of sorting out difficulties and miscommunications between workers and young people, it was immensely successful and well-regarded. However, at the formal level it was impossible through the whole period to get the complaints officer to accept a case as a formal complaint. Most often, this was because formal complaints were often about serious matters of organisational policy and managerial decision – such things as the closure of children's homes, for example, where by law (Children Act, 1989) the residents must be consulted. The agency, although very well-disposed to advocacy and effective complaints procedures, was unable to conceive of them as questioning fundamental policies and managerial decisions within the agency. The managers thought that supporting advocacy would prevent everyday problems in services blowing up into conflict, and so it did. But they presumed that the problems would be with the people they managed failing to meet the high standards they set, not with the policy and organisation of the agency itself. The hierarchy of their bureaucratic structure led them to assume there was a reverse hierarchy of advocacy. They thought there was less need for advocacy further up the hierarchy, because the purpose of advocacy is to ensure that the policy of the agency is properly implemented.

Here we see an example of the way in which managerialism perverts consumerism and user participation. Managerialism assumes that the purpose of user participation, and related services like advocacy, are to act as a check on the effectiveness of the organisation. They are not seen as a way of questioning the policy and purposes of the organisation, as defined by managers. Managerialism denies democratic arguments for participation, which say, for example, that citizens are entitled to a say in public services and decisions which affect them.

Another issue which arises from such experiences is the effect of advocacy services on workers. If managers behave as though the purpose of advocacy is to check on the worker, assuming that the policy and management of the organisation are untouchable, workers will resent and resist the introduction of advocacy. This might lead to extreme resistance to anything the advocacy scheme does. Alternatively, workers may, in effect, abdicate from responsibility for decisions, because their managers always accept the advocate's position on behalf of the user, or because they are not prepared or do not have the skills to accept the conflict or argue their position. Advocacy is a contribution to professional decision-making by making sure that the user's view is fully represented within it. It is not a substitute for or negation of professional responsibility.

In another similar project (Dalrymple and Payne, 1995), I found that managerial decisions like this, although clearly either illegal or counterproductive, were regarded within local authorities as completely unquestionable. Until, that is, in this case, the advocate came along. Then decisions questioned and argued against by clients and social workers for months were overturned after a few minutes' exposition by the advocate. I was forced into wondering why local authorities employ and pay social workers if they do not intend to take any notice of their judgement or the information they gain through their work with clients.

Most often, the apparent issue was one of discretion. The social worker had no discretion to spend the money, neither did their boss. However, the system of the local authority did not give them any access to someone who did have the discretion. Alternatively, sometimes arguing for discretion to be used discredited the regard in which workers and junior managers were held by their superiors. Therefore, they felt that it was better to find an independent person to put the case. So when the advocate rang up, a senior official immediately overturned clearly inappropriate decisions. However, this did not seem to lead to a review of the system for permitting discretion. The whole practice of the local authority went on obstructing sensible decisions in other cases, instead of learning from the case that the advocate took up.

This is one weakness of case advocacy which causes many campaigning organisations to turn to cause advocacy. Changing the decision in one case leaves unchanged the basic premises of policy which led to the bad decision. It is like the consequences of the managerialist position on advocacy, discussed above. Advocacy is seen as appropriate for righting the occasional failing, but the possibility that this demonstrated widespread failures in policy and management was not touched on by this case-by-case approach. However, this is also a failure of management, since most management writing would say that managers should use complaints procedures for identifying and correcting policy and management issues. Again, though, the assumptions which underlie that prescription suggest that the responsibility lies with the politicians and managers to decide what is right. It denies the potential influence of the citizens affected.

I came to the conclusion that the inflexible decision-making was really a part of the rationing process. If workers in contact with service users were given discretion, senior managers feared that they would exercise it in sensible ways which would lead them to overspend the budget. By not giving any discretion and obstructing sensible decisions as long as possible, the managers hoped that most of the demands for resources would fade away. Only the most persistent got through and had their needs met. Controlling professional discretion, then, is covertly about rationing. This emphasis on rationing completely perverts the managerialist agenda of responding to consumers' needs in the public sector. As we have seen, it is one pressure which has led social workers to reduce professional advocacy on behalf of their clients.

On the other hand, it is an inappropriate use of advocacy to 'second-guess' the worker, or to extend from advocacy into acting as a counsellor or alternative worker. For example, a mental health social worker was working with a patient who had been in hospital for some years. The only relative, a sister, remembered the disruption and fear that the patient had brought to her family when his illness was at its most serious. She feared that social work aimed at discharging the patient might rely on having him to live with her family. She was therefore resisting contacts with her family. Delicate negotiations and reassurances over some months by the social worker led to the sister resuming contact at the hospital. However, it was made clear to the patient in these negotiations that on discharge he would be placed in a hostel some way away. There was no prospect of his returning home. He approached an advocacy worker to appeal against this decision, seeking closer contact with his sister. The advocacy worker wrote to the sister asking for this on the patient's behalf, and this led to the sister breaking off all contact again, to the patient's disadvantage. Here, the advocate trespassed into the worker's task. The appropriate course was to represent the patient in a review of the decisions of the worker by her clinical team or by her managers. By acting directly, the advocate damaged the development of the work, to the detriment of the patient.

While this may seem obvious, advocates may easily be drawn into inappropriate relationships. Because they are always on the side of the user and do not actually have responsibility for the decisions or resources, they may seem more sympathetic. The requirement that advocacy achieves a good relationship of trust with the user may lead to the advocate being sucked into a counselling-style relationship. These shifts from the role of advocacy are not, however, necessary. If they are careful to define their roles well, both users and advocate will find it easy to maintain the separation of responsibilities between worker and advocate. One interesting finding of the child advocacy research was that young people clearly understood the distinction between the responsibilities of an advocate and that of their social worker (Dalrymple and Payne, 1995).

I have argued, then, that it is integral to the policy of much social provision that social workers should accept, within the balance of their roles, an ethical advocacy element. Managerial acceptance of this is essential to carrying out the policy of the guidance and legislation in nearly all the areas in which social workers work. Moreover, the professional role which social workers occupy and the only way of doing their job necessarily involves accepting a responsibility for advocacy. Finally, clients expect it, and it needs to be carried out honestly.

However, managerialised bureaucracies seem to find this hard to accept, so that we have to be clear what the requirements for advocacy as part of social work are.

Requirements for advocacy

As we saw in Chapter 2, having advocacy available is a basic requirement for a service which responds to service users' views and their wishes as consumers. Attitudes to this provision have, I have argued in this Chapter, developed so that advocacy by social workers on behalf of their clients has been played down. So, many social workers have come to see it as problematic in manageri-alised, bureaucratic services. The replacement for this is seen as external, user-led advocacy services. I would argue that these are not alternatives and that both must be available. Moreover, the two must interact. So we need three types of responses to advocacy as follows:

- advocacy by social workers for their clients
- advocacy services acting on behalf of service users
- positive responses by the agency to advocacy when it is used by service users, or by social workers on behalf of their clients (a 'culture of advocacy')

Social workers will always advocate for their clients. This is so because they hear the clients directly, and their job is to represent the clients' needs, feelings and views in the agency's decision-making processes. I mean here 'represent' in the sense of 'interpret'. The social work job involves writing case records, court reports, social histories, applications for services, making assessments, and plans and monitoring and evaluating their service. In all these ways social workers interpret their clients to the social services system. They will be doing this all the time; it is integral to the job; the skills are integral to training and competence in the job. It is possible to do it from the agency's point of view or another external perspective or from the client's point of view. Advocacy requires taking the client's view, but professional responsibility may mean including other perspectives, while not blunting the strength of the represen-tation of the client's position.

Advocacy services are needed for two situations. One is where users' views (and sometimes those of other interest groups') are represented and user control of expression of these views is important. This recognises that sometimes the responsibilities of a social worker are different from that of a service user. In child care matters, for example, social workers must pursue the 'best interests' of a child, whereas children are entitled to pursue their 'wishes and feelings'. Therefore, an advocacy service will routinely have to be sure that the child's rights to pursue their 'wishes and feelings' are taken into account. The worker, and case conferences and reviews that they attend, might scrupulously find out and consider the child's wishes and feelings. Even if they do this, the different requirements of their role may well be seen by the child or by others to conflict with their responsibilities. Advocacy services make sure that rights are *seen* to be respected. Having an advocacy service for the child also frees workers to focus on their responsibilities. It allows them to distinguish clearly when they are taking a 'best interests' decision as opposed to a 'wishes and feelings' decision. It also makes clear to all concerned when the child's wishes and feelings are overruled in their best interests. Without an advocacy service, workers sometimes feel that the child's best interests must always override their wishes and feelings, which then get unreasonably ignored.

The second situation where advocacy services are required is where matters of management, policy and planning affecting several or many users are involved. An example is in primary care groups or locality commissioning, where in the first instance family doctors' practices and in the second instance local groups and agencies in an area get together to work out user and community views on what services should be developed and commissioned. Here, it is effective for users to share in developing their own point of view. It prevents the need for managers or planners to make sense of a wide range of individual views. Moreover, it places users in control with collective responsibility for putting forward points of view to the agency. Otherwise, managers might choose the views that suit them and avoid the others: at least they may seem to do so. Another advantage is that involvement of users from the outset is likely to lead to a greater respect for and valuation of the services.

User participation and advocacy for their views, however, do not mean abdicating the workers' or agencies' responsibilities. For example, in one local authority Deaf people were consulted about priorities for sign-language interpreters. The authority gave a high priority to attending the court or police cells to aid the representation of Deaf people at risk of legal action or losing their liberty. However, this sometimes disrupted the routine provision of interpreters. The users felt that their doctors' and dentists' appointments should have priority because people in court or at the police station had 'done wrong'. The authority could not agree to this. However, the participation was important, because it revealed the dissatisfaction that users felt with present priorities, and allowed the authority to explain and justify their position. Going further, a cause advocate would suggest that it reveals inadequacy in resources, because funding should be enough for interpreters to meet routine needs as well as the criminal justice emergencies. An awareness of the advocacy role strengthens our ability to note and argue for correcting such hidden resource problems.

The final aspect of advocacy is the preparation of the organisation for advocacy, both by its own workers and by advocacy services. Advocacy by workers can be improved by making it clear at what points the information and judgements of workers representing clients' circumstances are included in decision-making, and by providing for an explicit decision about the judgements represented. So in decision-making it should be clear, for example, if the client has asked for occupational therapy at the day centre and the worker's assessment supports it. If it is rejected, the decision, the reasons and the responsibility for it should be clearly defined. Advocacy services need to be facilitated by training, information and management support. A team, for example, can bring together information to support the work of all its members, and organise joint training to cover areas where they think they should be advocating.

Is advocacy enough?

Advocacy is important, I have argued, for making social services less bureaucratic. This is because it sets out to provide explicit processes for the voices of users to be heard directly, presented in ways that retain the character of those voices instead of being interpreted through professional words and conventions. If users can see this happening, some of the problems of professional jargon and the oppressive feeling of bureaucratic procedures may be overcome. If this is well-established in an agency, workers can find acceptance of their discretion and judgement in the agency's decision-making processes. All this should make the agency more flexible and open to influence by the people who use its services.

There may be problems, however. If the organisation is bureaucratic anyway, there may be a tendency for advocacy to become bureaucratised, too. This is particularly so because advocacy is often procedural in character. It is, for example, concerned with formal representation in case conferences, reviews, or complaints procedures. It may be done in an informal relationship, but it needs to participate in more formal procedures which affect users. Because it applies pressure to managers and workers to act 'properly' and to be seen to do so, it may encourage proceduralism: putting everything in writing and following very formal processes, for example. So it may not have an anti-bureaucratic effect. Throughout this chapter, we have identified many problems and difficulties with making advocacy by professionals in their work, and advocacy services effective. They can be overcome, but this does not always happen.

Advocacy may also involve conflicts between different interests. I have written this chapter as though advocacy is only or mainly on behalf of users. However, workers are in complex relationships with a whole network of people in every case. Child care work might involve responsibilities for parents as well as children, foster carers and residential care workers as well as the child being looked after. In community care, a range of carers, neighbours, family members and community interests may come into play. For example, an elderly woman with Alzheimer's was being rehabilitated to a relative's home. However, neighbours nearby complained about the distress and inconvenience caused by her wandering and sometimes difficult behaviour in the street when she was last home. These prejudicial assumptions might be dismissed in professional decision-making, but it complicates the return home and adds to the distress for the elderly woman and her family. Moreover, it may lead to complaints to politicians or to the media about inappropriate decisions, which then need to be defended publicly. A process of education and reassurance, discussion and consultation with the neighbours was required, before the risk of discharge could be undertaken. A worker cannot just identify with one interest, that of the user's: to make what the user wants or needs work, they have to consider and respond to a range of other interests.

Another difficulty is that advocacy is very often used in exceptional circumstances, when something has gone wrong. Also, when workers interpret their clients' needs and argue on their behalf within the system it conflicts with the many other roles and responsibilities that they have. As a result, workers' roles become more complex and ambiguous within their daily work. Users, managers, politicians and others may undermine the possibility of using workers' advocacy because they cannot accept the lack of clarity in workers' roles within the agency's structure of accountability and therefore acknowledge their representative and interpretive role .

Responding more adequately to anti-bureaucratic practice, therefore, requires a greater range of responses than advocacy, and it is to this that we turn in the next Chapter.

Chapter 4
ANTI-BUREAUCRATIC PRACTICE

Anti-bureaucratic practice defined

What is anti-bureaucratic practice? We can define it partly through the problems that we experience in bureaucratic and managerialist behaviour. The first chapter examined problems of bureaucratic behaviour and why it appears in the social services. The second looked at how managerialism made these problems worse, as it was implemented in pursuit of new Right policies from the 1980s onwards. From these discussions, we can identify some anti-bureaucratic practice principles.

In Chapter 1 we saw that applying bureaucratic principles inflexibly achieved certainty, consistency and fairness but obstructed the agency's purposes for users. Procedures are set up to protect the agency and prevent things from going too wrong on behalf of service users. However, in bureaucratic behaviour the procedures became more important than the overall purposes the agency was trying to achieve. We need to be flexible and use discretion in following procedures and systems where they do not achieve the agency's purpose. On the other hand, we cannot avoid and ignore procedures which protect everyone in the cause of some ideal of flexibility. We must use the procedures to achieve quality objectives.

The easiest way of understanding this is that we should be genuinely needs-led. The needs that lead us should be those that our clients and service users define. We should also take into account the needs that reasonable people think we should achieve. I put in this proviso partly because service users are sometimes inarticulate or unreasonable about what they need. Then, needs have to be defined for them. I fear that often the social services define needs in ways which suit the services, rather than the users. The 'reasonable people's' purpose counters that tendency of official organisations. Countering it is important because low standards and poor quality objectives bring us into disrepute. 'Yes,' we can say, 'we do what the service standards set down'. But can we say that the standards are what we would ideally want? 'But,' we can say, 'people are not prepared to pay taxes to achieve the best standards.' Maybe, but when they come across the standards that we set, they very often think that we should be doing better for their friends and relatives. Therefore, we need to look carefully at achieving better standards even within the given resources.

In Chapter 2, we saw that managerialism is a politically motivated control mechanism which conflicts with basic principles of public sector management and services. Managerialism goes beyond bureaucratic control by procedures, in favour of control by performance indicators and budgets. Anti-bureaucratic practice aims to maintain the benefits of the public sector ideal while incorporating them into the effectiveness which good management practice offers. There is nothing wrong with well-defined objectives and controls to ensure that they are attained. However, such standards must not twist how we respond to individuals' needs. So we need to maintain the benefits of bureaucratic practice: neutrality, balance and fairness in accordance with public criteria for providing services. This seems just the opposite of attacking bureaucratic excess. I believe this is one reason that anti-bureaucratic social work seems so difficult. We feel we should avoid inflexibility, yet procedures are the basis of fairness and balance.

However, just as focusing on the user's needs and aims is the answer to bureaucratic inflexibility, openness and multiprofessionalism are answers to control-freak managerialism. Anti-bureaucratic practice is open, because fairness and neutrality require openness about the objectives that we are given and the conflicts that we face. It is multiprofessional, because corporate objectives mean that we have to practice together with colleagues in pursuit of shared objectives. Separate professional agendas and divided services obstruct meeting users' needs. Although this meets the managerialist agenda, it also meets what service users would want. They want to be treated as equals; they want us to cooperate for their benefit. They do not want hidden purposes and uncoordinated services. They do not want arrogant and individualistic professionals pursuing their prejudices: they want cooperation and coordinated services. Managerialism may have political and economic objectives that we might disagree with. Implemented on the ground, though, it demands only what most people would see as entirely reasonable. Perhaps that is why the managerialist attack on how public services are run has been so popular with the public, and is supported by political parties of all ideological persuasions.

'But,' you may say, 'it is only a cover for new Right political objectives and controlling resources.' Maybe, but the traditional political system tells us that the objectives of those elected to govern us must inform how public servants work. Most people think that the public sector wastes money, and are pleased to see resources properly controlled. We cannot object to these things. Still, we can be open about the operation of these factors and how they affect particular individuals. Most service users are pleased that resources are carefully managed and husbanded. They prefer to understand why decisions are made as they are. They do not want more than their due, but they want as much as is their due. They want it to be evidently fair. Also, as we have seen in Chapter 3, they are entitled to seek the best they can, through our advocacy, and through the benefits of advocacy services. They cannot do that, unless we are open about how and why decisions are being made as they are.

My definition of anti-bureaucratic practice, then, incorporates three elements. *Anti-bureaucratic practice within the context of a managed agency focuses on achieving, flexibly, needs defined by service users through multi-professional interventions which are openly agreed with service users, offering resources which are fairly employed and distributed.* This definition is represented in Figure 4.1. Here we see professionals and service users operating in partnership to define and focus on the users' definitions of needs. As a result, multiple professions are involved cooperatively in employing and distributing resources. Users are further enabled by professionals accepting their responsibility for advocacy, and by the availability of advocacy services to represent users within the system. However, all this takes place within a managed agency: it allows us to incorporate the political and policy objectives and accountability for efficiency and effectiveness represented by responsibility to managers within the bureaucratic structure.

Figure 4.1 Anti-bureaucratic practice

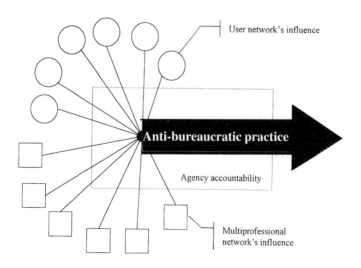

In the remainder of this Chapter, I want to look at what the anti-bureaucratic practice approach might mean as we go about trying to implement it.

Anti-bureaucratic practice is genuinely needs-led

Being anti-bureaucratic seems like a good idea, so why do we not all do it instantly? There are several answers. On our own, we cannot fight the bureaucratic world as it is. We saw in Chapter 1 that bureaucratic systems have advantages, lost because of the British system, which we want to regain. We cannot go against the entirely legitimate trend towards looking at our effectiveness and practising to achieve more for our clients and service users. Instead, I have suggested, we must incorporate it in our work, without allowing management for effectiveness to become managerialised over-bureaucracy.

So, how can we understand anti-bureaucratic practice? We have to avoid seeing it as a fight against everything bad in the organisations we work in. All organisations have bad aspects, and always will. We need a practical interpretation of anti-bureaucratic practice, in the context of present-day social services. Therefore, the starting point has to be benefit for clients and service users. Nobody can argue against this objective; it is the underlying purpose of 'needs-led' services.

As an example, Diana is a young woman of fourteen, whose disturbed and inadequate behaviour when she was thirteen led her school to refer her to the psychological service. She was bright, but not making the best of school because she could not develop relationships with others, seemed lost in a fantasy life, and often reacted aggressively or in a peculiar manner. The psychological assessment revealed a need for treatment. Diana had several placements, but deteriorated fast, going on psychotropic medication in order to control her behaviour. Eventually, she ended up accommodated in a residential care home in voluntary care because her parents could not cope with her disturbed behaviour at home. However, the parents were committed to her and visited frequently, staying overnight on many weekends. There was a considerable improvement, with Diana coming off psychotropic medication. On the whole, the residential home managed outbursts of difficult behaviour. However, Diana was not doing much in special education. Staff at the residential care home felt that the parents' involvement was disrupting Diana's stability, because the parents' treatment of Diana was inevitably different from the staff approach. They therefore proposed a reduction or hiatus in parental visiting. At a case conference, the parents protested that they wanted to maintain their involvement with their daughter consistently and she appeared to want this. This was regarded as non-cooperation. However, the social worker felt forced to support the residential care home, because it was impossible for Diana to return home, and the service needed to make best use of an expensive resource. The parents, on the other hand, felt excluded. They argued that that since Diana had a continuing relationship with them she would feel rejected if they reduced their involvement. Also, they wanted to maintain their support at this time as the basis for providing future care. The residential home staff took to documenting events in which the parents seemed to get in the way of what they were seeking to achieve.

This complex situation is not commonplace, but it includes many recurring features which force us to work bureaucratically. First, what is bureaucratic about this case? The people involved would say they are operating on a very individualised basis, with careful and professional assessments of the situation at every turn. The events are uncommon, so the reaction is not routinised. Considerable resources are being expended: certainly they are not taking the cheap option. Some success has finally been achieved: surely this should be supported and pushed forward.

However, if we look closely, several 'bureaucracies' are relevant. First, we are here operating the care system and offering its provisions, but we are not achieving reasonable objectives. This is often hidden from us by the difficulty of the situations that we face: it all seems so difficult that gaining anything seems like progress. However, thinking about the users' aims and the reason-able person's expectations, achievement has been poor. Diana has been involved in the 'system' for some time. In a year, someone who was a bit strange but recognisably bright at an ordinary school has undergone disastrous treatment, serious deterioration and is only now being recovered from this. Things may be improving now, but frankly an outsider would say that the 'system' contributed to the deterioration in the first place. Because the parents have problems in caring for the young person, the assumption is that the 'system' is the right or only provision. Parental involvement is disrupting the 'system', so the 'system' must be supported. The worker feels that she must support her colleagues against the outsiders (the 'clients' they are supposed to be helping). Also, because there is no alternative, the care home's needs must be regarded as more important than what the young person or parents want.

This is bureaucracy because maintaining the 'system' and the courtesies within it becomes more important than the individuals involved. Moreover, the approach here ignores the requirements of public policy, the legislation and best quality practice. These mean that the 'wishes and feelings' of the child (no matter how disturbed) must be considered seriously and her 'best interests' pursued. It cannot be in the young person's best interests to miss contact with her parents, whatever the inconvenience to the residential care home.

Continuing contact with parents is a high priority. The workers have been twisted into not thinking about this. Now Diana is in the 'system', defined as a problem, and cannot cope in 'normal life', they assume that the 'system's' requirements take over. Yet a year ago, this child, while not problem-free, was more-or-less-coping in normal life.

Part of the reason for this is the second element of bureaucracy here, the cost of the provision. Why take the child's and parents' view, when we are paying for expensive treatment? Yet what are we offering here? Diana gains a few sessions with a psychiatrist – not more frequently than an hour a week probably, if that. The advantage of regular contact with residential care staff is often limited by their lack of experience and qualifications and constantly changing shift patterns. They are under the direction of qualified, experienced and caring people no doubt, and perhaps there is a carefully devised treatment plan to guide them. Still, are we really preferring not to disrupt that in favour of cutting out the parents, who want to be involved and whose child wants them there? The parents and child are involved for the long term. We hope we are only there for a brief period of help. It is our job to facilitate the parents no matter how difficult they are, not get them to fit in with our convenience. Again, the needs of the service have taken primacy over the needs of the child and parents.

The anti-bureaucratic social work view of 'needs-led' services means starting from the individuals involved: how they define what they want and how a reasonable observer would define what they need. This is the ideal of needs-led services anyway, so how is anti-bureaucratic practice different? Of course, part of the answer is that having needs-led services is far from the truth of how things really happen in the social services, as this case has shown.

Gold, bronze and silver standard practice

The anti-bureaucratic practice answer to this problem is the gold, bronze and silver standards, shown in Figure 4.2. Very often our practice is forced to be at the bronze level: the absolute minimum that the agency can get away with to meet the needs. If this is all that can realistically be provided, we often ask ourselves: what is the point of thinking about anything better? There are two answers to this. First, if we think about the gold standard, what we might ideally provide, we have something to aim at. It might give us ideas about things we could do, that we otherwise might ignore. In particular, by consulting carefully with clients, service users, their carers and others involved, we can always find a way in which the situation could be made better for them. By using this information, we can make an unsatisfactory situation seem better for them.

This leads to the next and crucial point. Secondly, *we can always do better than the bronze standard*, so we can always get to a silver standard. How is this possible? The answer is that we can always make the experience of even the minimum level of provision feel more satisfying to the service user.

Figure 4.2 Gold, silver and bronze standard practice

	Standard	*Definition*
	Gold	The best level of service which would be provided if there were no cost or practical constraints.
	Silver	The acceptable level of service which enhances quality of service within cost and practical constraints.
	Bronze	The minimum level of service adequate to deal with the identified needs, within the required cost and practical limits.

As in Diana's case, the issue is very often not only about resources. Bureaucracy places the 'system' and its maintenance above the needs of the service user. Not evidently but subtly, our response to people changes as we regard them as the problem which the system has to cope with. Instead, we should see the problems that we identify jointly as the issues that we jointly have to face. Bureaucracy sets us against our clients, because it places the needs of the organisation first. This is more obvious where the issue is resources. In many community care assessments, we end up providing only the bronze standard because we do not have the resources to provide it.

In Diana's case, it feels as if we are doing more than the bronze standard, because we are spending so much money on an expensive resource. There has also been some success in improving her behaviour. Look again, though, at the original objectives of involvement. These parents, if they had articulated it, would have wanted their bright daughter to fulfil her potential in school and play her full part in their family. Most of all both they and she wanted herself to be happy. These objectives, sought by the school in the original referral, which the parents or any outsider not caught up in the situation would set, define our gold standard. Perhaps the social worker can congratulate herself on finding a placement that recovered deterioration. Overall, though, the situation has got worse, in spite of the entirely reasonable objectives that the parents and child must have started with.

So we are at the bronze standard here. We have a placement which is doing some good, and she is in school, but not achieving anything. How can we get ourselves towards the gold standard? There are two possibilities. One is to improve Diana's achievement at, and involvement with, a school which is appropriate to her capability. The other is to improve her functioning in relation to her parents, producing a happier family which can integrate Diana again into their midst. Keeping Diana in residential care, separating her from her parents, and in a special school with aimless provision does not move towards either of these entirely reasonable objectives. An active programme of identifying her talents at school and fulfilling them at all costs might not achieve the gold standard, but it is better than now. An active programme of working with the parents and Diana might not result in an ideal family, but it must be better than now. That is the silver standard.

Let us look at a more obvious case. Mrs Green is a widow in her eighties, isolated and a long way from any close family, somewhat disabled, and house-bound through fear of falling. There have been two admissions to hospital, which she likes because it is safe. At her home, she gets twice-daily home help, assistance with personal hygiene and minor medical treatments from a district nurse. Aids have been supplied and various adaptations made to the house. Mrs Green would happily stay in hospital, but the bed is needed. She would agree to a nursing home and residential care but she is not high priority. She rejects meals on wheels ('not as good as the hospital's, dear') so nutrition is not too good because Mrs Green cannot be bothered with anything requiring much effort. As with Diana, good resources have been provided, but in this case no more than the minimum necessary. It is routine provision really; thousands are like this. The bronze standard, then, is what we provide to the Mrs Greens of this world: not inadequate, but not the best, because if she had the money there is no doubt she would go into a home. So, if that is the gold standard, what is there that she would gain? Most of all, she would gain freedom from fear – of falling. She would also gain relief from isolation through some resident social life, and might even gain the opportunity to go out sometimes, in an organised and supportive way. She would also achieve better nutrition, probably. A social worker would probably be dubious about the benefits of a home, since many do not provide stimulating and safe care but are merely holding institutions which are not very pleasant. Nevertheless, that does not alter the fact that in the ideal (the gold standard) it would be a good experience for Mrs Green. However, we could do things in the present situation to improve Mrs Green's experience in many of these areas. We can imagine volunteer visitors, trips out, day care and call systems. They might not require many extra resources, provided we have organised for such things to be available in her area. Perhaps she needs to be put in touch with some local groups; such contacts are pretty much universal. Still, we are doing well enough, and the expectation of a home for everyone is unrealistic. So it is, but we can still improve on the bronze standard if we want to. Anti-bureaucratic social work says we should want to.

Working with organisations and causes
In other circumstances, we might be focusing, as with advocacy, on causes rather than or as well as cases. Concern with cases will lead us mainly to focus anti-bureaucratic practice on service users. Concern with causes will probably lead us mainly to focus on organisations, our own or those of other service providers. This distinction is not complete, however. Focusing on changing organisations may bring the best result for a user. Bringing up a range of cases might point to the need for change, or we could help a group of users seek change. However, we need to be aware of the ethical element in this decision. We should not neglect a user's immediate need to achieve a longer-term objective. Also, we should not misuse, without permission and the user's knowledge and involvement, our work with a user for wider purposes. This also has a practical reason: user participation is often effective in influencing change in an organisation. From the user's point of view, they will learn ways of influencing organisations which might help them. Therefore, involvement in the anti-bureaucratic process in the present can help them in the future.

Looking first at the broader role of organisations, we might focus on change in our own organisation or in others; both might be possible. We also need to consider if we are going to target policies which are about how the organisation understands and interprets particular problems or issues. An alternative is to focus on practices: that is how the organisation deals with people. It is easy to improve a dull reception area and do a hundred minor things that improve how our service is experienced. Easy moves like these can have as big an impact for users as changing some policies.

Turning to anti-bureaucratic work with users, we need to consider whether we want to focus on one service user or on all users or on a group of them. For example, a colleague wanted to raise greater awareness of response to ethnic minority group needs in a residential care home. He became aware of the issue through the experience of an African Caribbean resident he was working with. However, after talking it over with the resident, he judged that it was better to approach it by raising the general issue through the staff team. At the same time, he worked with several ethnic minority residents for them to raise issues concerning them. This took the heat off his particular client.

While working with service users, we might want to look at outcomes, decisions or what the service provides. Alternatively, how the service 'feels' to users and the attitudes conveyed in practice may be more important. So the 'quality' of our practice arises from both specific outcomes and how we go about doing our work in general. I mean quality both in the sense of the indefinable something that users experience when becoming involved in a service and in the sense of meeting high standards. An example might be whether the agency behaves with integrity. Notice this word: it is related to 'integrated'; it implies that how we act integrates with what we say. If our service has integrity, it will be more evidently trustworthy to users. One way of achieving this is not to make promises that we cannot keep. The problem with following this principle is that resource allocation may be so uncertain, that we do not feel we can make *any* promises. This is bureaucratic because, to users, it feels like concealment of what is going on. So rather than avoiding promises, integrity contributes to service quality and anti-bureaucratic practice, with openness about what we are doing and thinking. This is so, even if it leads to users understanding and experiencing something of our uncertainty.

Anti-bureaucratic practice is open and multiprofessional
Integrity's contribution to the quality of our services means that *openness* is crucial to users feeling good about our services. What do we mean when we say that anti-bureaucratic practice is open? Most professionals like to think that they are open about what they are doing when they work in partnership with service users. However, here we are talking about a special kind of openness, which many professionals try to avoid. Openness in anti-bureaucratic practice means openness about the inflexibilities and hidden purposes of managerialism. Some people might question whether we should be open about these, and there are two fundamental criticisms: disloyalty to your organisation and employer, and confusing the service user by inconsistencies which might be oppressive.

First, let us consider the loyalty argument. This proposes that we should not reveal the inconsistencies and difficulties in the agency's work to outsiders – no washing dirty linen in public. However, service users are not outsiders: they are being provided with services, so they are part of us. This is their agency; the workers or the managers do not own it, neither do the politicians, the local authority nor the committee of management. The agency *is* owned by the private sector owner or shareholders whom a board might represent, but the service is not theirs: the service is for the user. Usually it is only too obvious when things have gone wrong or what the users want is not being provided. Also, we all know that things go wrong; we know that organisations generate inconsistencies and conflicts. Service users know that just as well as we do.

They can see when workers are being tactful about something that is wrong in the organisation and they respect this to a certain extent. When the worker overdoes this, it puts him or her on the organisation's side and not on the user's side. In any case, being open about bureaucratic inflexibilities does not set you against your agency. It helps to put you, the user and the organisation on the same side: trying to sort out whatever is getting in the way of providing the right service. The agency wants it, the worker wants it, the user wants it: they are all on the same side.

The second argument against openness is that it is oppressive for the user, because it faces them with all the obstructions and difficulties which the worker should be smoothing away. In answer to this, I am not advocating telling users about every minor problem that might come up, or informing them in detail of every step. Usually, this is not needed: they expect the worker to get on with it. However, being clear about the major aspects of what needs to be done helps the user take responsibility and prevents the user becoming anxious. We shall see this in some of the examples of openness that I discuss below.

Two final points about openness are reminders:

- Anti-bureaucratic social work does not only involve our own organisation. It also involves working with the user on the bureaucracies of other organisations, and the problems of links between organisations. Therefore, again, being silent about the obstructions and problems means being on the side of the system instead of being on the side of the user. It is the user's life and the user's service; the user should be involved in work on getting the service sorted out if bureaucracies are getting in the way.

- Anti-bureaucratic social work focuses on the basic purposes and aims of the agency, not on the procedures and policies which are proxies for it; they are convenient, consistent and generally reasonable stand-ins for the objectives, not the objectives themselves. The rules and procedures are there to implement political and managerial policies. However, if they get in the way of achieving the results that the policies want, it is the worker's duty to work round them and to seek to change them. If there is a conflict between procedures and objectives, the worker's loyalty should be to the objectives, not the procedures.

Anti-bureaucratic practice will, therefore, focus on purposes and users' needs, to test whether the procedures and performance indicators are achieving what is required.

Substantive not procedural equality

The problem of bureaucracy is that its top-down approach to authority does not match well with modern social movements which require diversity, flexibility, openness and participation. It says, in effect, that maintaining the appearance of fairness and equality by treating everyone the same (procedural equality) is more important than being able to argue that the outcome is right for the people concerned (substantive equality). However, procedural equality does have advantages. Our aim, in anti-bureaucratic practice, therefore, is to preserve bureaucracy's neutrality, certainty and clarity and combine it with concern for outcomes. We saw in Chapter 2 that neutrality, certainty and clarity through procedural fairness do not always lead to substantive justice. However, the fear of managements is the loss of control, and the impact of managerialism makes this worse, because that is an approach to management which emphasises control. While seeking anti-bureaucratic practice, therefore, we are likely to come up against the pressures of managerialism.

We saw, in Chapter 2, on the other hand, that managerialism does not sit well with public services. By focusing on the positive aspects of public service organisations, we work against the undesirable aspects of managerialism. Therefore, we would want to emphasise fairness, participation, diversity and flexibility – substantive equality rather than procedural equality. This means dealing with outcomes comprehensively and, often, multiprofessionally. Bureaucracy leads to dividing up the problem and making decisions according to restrictive and restricted procedures.

Purposes and outcomes, not procedures
This requires us to look at the substantive rather than the procedural in working with our own agency and others. The bureaucratic approach to management applies established rules, approved by authority, as conventions to implement the purposes and aims of the agency. However, as we saw in Chapter 1, those purposes are set down in legislation, political policies and, for voluntary organisations, the constitution or memorandum and articles of association. They are more powerful then the procedures which are offshoots of the original purposes. We should identify the primary agency purposes from mission and policy statements, or from common sense and use these as levers against formally organised authority in agencies.

For example, a colleague deals with discharging mentally ill people from hospital. All the plans might be made and housing applied for. Housing associations are subject to policy imperatives which seek to reduce the time that property is vacant – this is more efficient, does not lose rent income, does not waste housing. So, when a housing allocation is made, the property must be seen within a few days, accepted there and then (or not, but this reduces the possibility of getting a further allocation), and rent is charged from within a week. However, the worker has to make application for housing benefit, for social security allowances, and a community care grant, which can only be paid when the house is known. Therefore, the mentally ill person is likely to enter the property with no furniture or equipment, not even a kettle to make tea. Several weeks later, they will have accumulated a huge rent and community charge bill which will then always be in arrears. Only if the worker is very persistent will all this be sorted out; most clients in this position do not get that persistent help. The little brown envelopes constantly arriving are likely to push a delicately balanced, mentally ill person over the edge, no matter how much the social worker reassures the former patient. This does not achieve the purpose of the housing association, the government, the health service, the SSD, the worker or the patient.

Neither side is unreasonable, though. The policy is a sensible one for many purposes, but it makes for problems in particular instances of discharge from hospital. The approach, therefore, needs to emphasise the reasonableness of the main policy, yet identify a class of exceptions which anyone will find very hard to argue against. In sorting out the problems in particular cases through case advocacy, the worker might mention to workers in other parts of the system how difficult this rule is proving. Reports to managers might be made, suggestions for policy meetings put up. Evidence is needed of examples of the problems and how easily they might be sorted out. The answer might come from changes in housing allocation policy for mentally ill people, or more broadly people being discharged from hospital, or more broadly still people being discharged from all sorts of institutions. Alternatively, the answer might come from special arrangements for social security allowances to cover people in this position.

We have to understand the bureaucratic system in doing this kind of work. Individual arrangements can usually be made by workers on the ground or by members of the public. Classes of exceptions usually require a managerial decision; the question is: at what level? If the housing association can make the change without affecting their general achievement of their performance targets, a low-level management decision might be made. However, if the problem is common enough to affect the performance targets, policy decisions might be needed at the top of the organisation. Alternatively, efforts might be made to change the Housing Corporation's targets set for housing associations in general. If this is impossible because of political pressure, political campaigning will be needed. The same applies when taking the social security path in achieving the outcome we want. Officials on the ground can sort individual arrangements out. Special arrangements for a group, say for a hospital closing a ward which will lead to many discharges, might be made by managers. Getting the rules changed to apply to all hospital discharges will need the accumulation of advocacy successes, policy lobbying and perhaps, political campaigning.

Decisions and actions: quality outcomes, not correct processes
If we are to escape from the tyranny of procedure, we have to understand why proceduralism seems so important. In a managerialised bureaucracy, an important aspect of proceduralism is to gain public acceptance of decisions. This especially applies to decisions which might be disputed, such as rationing decisions. The bureaucracy can claim that, because of its neutral, certain and clear procedures, decision-making in transparently fair. However, this is to elevate procedural equality above substantive equity, an option which we have already rejected. Hence, we must look beyond procedural fairness to the content of decisions and the effect that they have on service users and their lives.

We have to ask: 'What is the impact of our decisions and actions on the client's life and the life of their community around them? What is the impact on a service which should be coordinated with related professionals and services?' The question is not only whether there is an impact, but whether the impact is desirable, and who measures what is desirable. It is important not to forget effects on 'the community'. Quality work needs to gain the respect of people in the community. Social service users are not separate from the people who surround them. What happens to them and what we provide needs to gain general support.

An example is the case of Catherine, a child being looked after by the local authority, because of abuse by her father, (who has been in prison for some time). Her mother would like both the child and the husband back in the home. The SSD decided that the child would not be returned home to a house where the husband also lived. The husband was not prepared to cooperate with sex offender work in the prison. However, the probation officer was keen for him to return to the home, to improve stability after discharge from prison. The mother was depressed and anxious and receiving treatment from a local community mental health team. The psychiatrist was anxious to improve her condition and thought that the reunion of the family, at least Catherine's return, would be the best option. Local people were opposed to the return of the husband, being angered by his behaviour towards Catherine, and fearing for the safety of their own children. This is the sort of complex situation which many social workers get involved with. Which of the interests, Catherine's, the mother's, the father's, the community's should be most important? The child care social worker would say the child's needs are paramount. Others might agree, but the mother and the father also have needs which other workers have a duty to meet; meeting them might also help the child. Very often, professional groups go into combat with one another on behalf of their client, instead of looking at the situation in the round. The psychiatrist may not have high regard for the legal and social pressures on the SSD to protect the child. The child care worker will give priority to the child's best interests. The probation officer might understand all this, but knows that the father will be released whatever other services wish, and may move back to the house in secret. Settling the father and preventing further offences both require some open arrangement to be arrived at. The mental health team want to facilitate the mother's improvement.

Each professional could go ahead with what they want to do for their own client's interest. The child protection worker could have a conference and agree that the child will not be allowed home unless the mother promises not to have the husband in the house. It protects the child, but this is bureaucracy because it does not take account of any of the consequences, or help to resolve them. As bureaucracy often does, it divides up the problems, according to professionals' and agencies' needs, rather than see them in their full context from the clients' points of view. This action foists the stress of the decision on the mother, and may damage improvement in her health. Will the father have a proper explanation and be helped to decide what to do for his own benefit and his daughter's? If there has been good preparation and working together, perhaps he might be moved towards taking action to deal with his sexual behaviour. That might be a quality decision for all concerned. However, if he is pushed into that without full understanding and confrontation of the need for change, he may go through the motions, but there will not be the decrease in risk that is hoped for. So he needs careful joint work between the prison, the probation officer and the child protection worker. If there is a decrease in risk, the neighbours and potential victims of further sexual abuse need to be confronted. They need to see that their concerns are taken seriously, and to understand why the professionals think the risk has been reduced. If they do not accept this, alternative placements or actions may be needed. In complex situations, quality decisions and actions involve all the aspects which will be affected. Unless they are all considered and acted upon, the quality of the outcome will be unsatisfactory.

I learned to oppose dividing up problems into competing perspectives when it was my job to set up residential care homes for recovering mentally ill people. Almost inevitably, our application for planning permission led to a neighbourhood campaign against us, and I attended meetings to hear the concerns of 'the community'. I would spend hours discussing how things would be organised and how safety would be assured. If I did not do this, our residents, when they finally arrived, would be subjected to much greater stress and difficulty in integrating themselves in the community. The bureaucratic option was to rely on the presumption of planning being in favour of providing such facilities. However, the quality response for residents involved taking the time and confronting the concerns. The neighbours needed to hear from the doctors, the social workers, the psychologists, the community nurses about how it was going to be. Usually, they accepted the outcome with varying levels of concern, and were pleasantly surprised when the residents arrived. They were made most angry by denials that there would be problems, and claims that we would manage everything well. They knew that people with mental illnesses would present problems, otherwise they would not need care. They knew that agencies, with the best will in the world, sometimes do not get it right. Reassurance was inappropriate; introducing them to how it would happen was effective.

Miranda is a young mother, sexually abused in childhood herself, with two children on the 'at- risk' register. She is, not surprisingly, bearing in mind these experiences of life, liable to severe depression and suicide attempts, often aimed at gaining support and help for herself and her family. A psychiatric hospital team from some way away deals with her, but the local mental health services will not accept her on to their caseload. She is not a high priority, because they give greater emphasis to people with the more severe psychoses. Episodes of depression can, in their view, be handled by the hospital. Yet her children are being dealt with by a child protection team in the same department. Both children and their workers would benefit from close involvement with more consistent treatment for the mother. This is bureaucracy again. One set of priorities is given precedence, without considering the wider issues and the full situation. Consequently, decisions and services do not aim for the best quality outcome for all involved.

The characteristic of many such situations is that the complexities of human lives mean that decisions affect several different issues in clients' lives, and agencies and professionals face inconsistent priorities. Anti-bureaucratic social work interprets the situation with an eye for high quality outcomes, not just for some of those involved but for all. A crucial element of this is the need to negotiate what should be done among different services and different professionals. Of course, each must focus on their priority task. However, unless they negotiate among them all towards an agreed satisfactory conclusion, the quality of the outcome will be wanting for some, and that poor quality will affect all.

Clarity, not obfuscation

One advantage of bureaucracy is the clarity that it brings to the way the organisation is set up and the way decisions are made. Two related aspects of clarity bring up some issues we have already identified that need particular attention in anti-bureaucratic social work: openness in making decisions and avoiding formality. Openness is required to make it clear to people how and why the decisions have been made the way they were. If we take the cheaper option because there are not enough resources, the service user needs to know that, and the priorities need to be open. Users are not fools: they can see that others might be in a worse position than they are, and they have just as much experience as the worker, if not more, of not being able to afford something. If they are entitled to appeal, then they should not have that right limited by not being told clearly why the decision was made. Either it can be justified or it cannot. If it can be justified, appeal will uphold the decision, clarify it and give it greater force for the user. It will also strengthen the worker and the agency. If it cannot be justified, appeal will restore rights and opportunities which the user rightly possesses.

Lack of openness hides in all sorts of conventional bureaucratic behaviour. For example, one of the things which we are quite often told is: 'We cannot do that: it would set a precedent'. There are two answers to this statement: 'Why?' and 'Why not?' Regarding the 'why?', we are dealing with an individual case and arguing for an individual's needs to be met. If there is good reason for this, on the basis of that individual, it need never set a precedent because it is based on that individual alone. Other people's circumstances will be different. On the other hand, referring to the 'why not?', if that individual's circumstances are the same as others', we will be setting a precedent and it is right that we should do so, if these circumstances justify providing a service or taking the proposed action. If we say we cannot do it because we might set a precedent, we are arguing one of two ways:

- that we have not collected the evidence to be clear that this special need is different from others' needs

- that the fact that provision is appropriate should be concealed from others who are just as entitled to the service.

Moreover, in this second case we are also saying that the service should be denied to this person not because they do not need the service but because it might reveal that others are entitled to it too. So a commonplace bureaucratic argument about setting a precedent really reveals a lack of openness in order to make things more convenient for ourselves.

Formality of language and in interpersonal behaviour with service users is bureaucratic for two reasons. One is that many people do not come across formal and legalistic language very much in their lives. Similarly, most of their experience of life is of relatively informal behaviour. Many people associate formality with officialdom and the use of authority against them: the experience is with the teacher, the policeman, the tax inspector. Therefore, legalistic language and formal behaviour can be frightening or confusing, so it discourages them from following up things that may be important. Formality also retains our own feeling of power. We seem so much more important and professional because we understand all this complicated language. However, behaving formally requires judgement: to some people it is pompous, to others it can be respectful. Moreover, using formal language and behaving formally hide our fear. We fear, perhaps, that we do not really understand the terms we are using or that we do not know how to behave or what to do. If we explain it clearly, perhaps the client will ask: 'Why is it like that then?' and we will not have an answer. If we are too informal, perhaps they will take advantage. Perhaps there is no answer. Perhaps, we do not explain it clearly because our policy is unjustifiable. Perhaps there are no resources to do what anyone can see we ought to do. Perhaps we set out by explaining it well and coping with all the questions and complaints, but after the tenth time of explaining to people, we take the easy way out and retreat to the formula explanation. Perhaps it is satisfactory for many people, but for some it will not be enough or appropriate. In anti-bureaucratic social work, there are no formulas (I don't say formulae, because although it would be strictly correct in the original Latin, readers are more likely to misunderstand it – that's anti-bureaucracy for you).

Secondly, formal and legalistic language is a secret language, so it conceals information. Moreover, it does so dishonestly because we give the impression of being open, of providing information, but actually we are hiding it. I shall always remember a vivid example of this kind of behaviour from a very senior social services official in my early career. I was on a working party looking at various child care procedures in my social services department, led by the Deputy Director. We reviewed and rewrote some letters sent out to parents whose children were (what would now be called) looked after by the local authority. One of these explained, hidden by a veil of legalistic language, how the charge was assessed and how parents could appeal against the charging decision. The Deputy Director looked at our rewritten version of the letter. 'You can't send this out,' he said: 'If you set it out this clearly, they'll *all* appeal.' I think it is rare for anyone, particularly in modern times, to be so open about the sheer obstructiveness of bureaucratic language, but I think this obstructiveness is often a hidden motivation in some of our behaviour. We make it easy for ourselves by giving someone who is not good with words the report to read, even though we know they will not understand its implications. We mouth the formal explanation, but do not take the trouble to make sure that people really understand it.

Using legalese and formality to dominate and conceal, therefore, avoids the professional job of social workers: interpreting the world to people who have difficulty with it and interpreting those people to a world that does not trouble to understand and respond to them. However, you can be too open, and this is equally bureaucratic. Have you seen a client's eyes glaze over as you try to give them the whole picture of what might happen to them in court or in a case conference? Have you ever gone into the routine of explaining something, and found yourself using the standard words and jargon? You have found yourself in robot mode, and that means you have lost interest in the real person in front of you. Being patronising in giving information or explanation has just the same effect. The client knows you are oversimplifying it in some way which is not geared to them as a person, but to your assumption about their low-level capacity to understand you.

Equally, arguing that we should avoid legalese and official sorts of explanations does not mean being careless about people's rights and duties. Because social workers operate on the boundaries of officialdom and the law, the issue is again our role in interpreting one to the other. We deal in the legal and official demands made on people, by our agencies and by others. So we cannot avoid dealing with legal matters, and if we are going to be open and responsible, we have to be correct and respectful in doing so. Anti-bureaucratic practice which respects legal rights and duties means pursuing our legal rights and responsibilities, and ensuring that our clients can pursue theirs. This also means that we must stick to the rules which defend and help them, just as they must meet their responsibilities and receive their rights. This brings us to the issue of the problems that arise over compliance with procedures.

Cooperation, not compliance
Bureaucratic behaviour and managerialist controls try to ensure consistent compliance with the requirements of authority. Compliance is often taken to mean going along with whatever instructions are given, without exercising any judgement. Clearly, this is not what any employer of professional people intends. Providers of social work services obviously expect workers to use their judgement in the situations they deal with. Anti-bureaucratic practice,

therefore, asks what the purposes of compliance are in each instance where it is expected. There are advantages in participation in rather than opposition to the bureaucratic system. We do not want to get lost in constant battles with the system – this will not gain our users their services. Also, there are advantages in organised, consistent systems. Organised systems and procedures do not cover all eventualities, however: they are not intended to. Many situations require thoughtful judgement. Do we need to seek the right to wide professional discretion to counter the inflexibilities of managerialised bureaucracies?

My answer to this question is 'no', for two main reasons. First, compliance is often justified. There is 'good' compliance and 'bad' compliance. It goes back to the fundamental point about anti-bureaucratic social work that we must focus on the objectives, not the procedures. 'Good' compliance means pursuing the requirements of the fundamental purposes and political policies of the agency. 'Bad' compliance means following procedures where they damage the particular case we are dealing with. Is this a recipe for anarchy, for professionals to do what they like if they judge the rules inappropriate to their case? Again, 'no'. Non-compliance does not mean just ignoring what we are required to do; anti-bureaucratic social work presses us to confront what is wrong and argue against it. As we have seen, at the level of the individual case, we may be seeking reasoned exceptions; at the level of a category of problems, we may be seeking a change of procedure; at the level of an injustice, we may be campaigning for political change. In the individual case, therefore, it is up to us to make the case that the procedure is wrong here, and to justify an exception. This should not be a commonplace grind, because if the procedure evidently does not work for many cases, it should be quickly changed.

Nonetheless, it is dangerous just to ignore a procedure that does not work. We often get round things by ignoring them, and it is dangerous for us and dangerous for service users. It means that service users lose the protection afforded to them by knowing that officials will comply with the rules. As we saw in Chapter 1, that method involves the risk of financial misbehaviour or worse. The inquiry into the 'Pindown' scandal (Levy and Kahan, 1991) found that good practice and legal protection for children in secure accommodation were ignored. There was some misconduct and poor resources but many people involved just drifted into avoiding the controls. The fact that there was a scandal and an inquiry in that case illustrates to workers the risk of non-compliance: they can be blamed for the failures that result.

The second leverage against unthinking compliance is cooperation. If we are cooperative and helpful to others, we can test the compliance which is required against whether it is positive for helpfulness. We can also set up an alternative mode of behaviour – reflective cooperation. So we do not set ourselves up against the rules and procedures, instead, we argue how they do not work in this case and we seek to get agreement to changes. We want to cooperate, but we want to negotiate a change for the better.

Of course, sometimes you do not get change that way: bureaucracies can be intransigent. Nevertheless, seeking change cooperatively is a prerequisite to other ways of pressing a case. Getting other agencies or users to complain, lobbying, political pressure, trade union action; all require cooperation. They might be seen as more extreme forms of action, but they are available, they are legitimate, if used properly, and they can help to achieve change.

I have not, so far, emphasised the multiprofessional element of anti-bureaucratic social work, though it appears in many of the examples I have given. Bureaucracy fails because of the complexity of normal life, the relatively structured sets of rules sanctioned by authority. Complex cases usually involve more than one agency and more than one professional. I have argued for cooperation, for negotiation around the range of issues to achieve quality outcomes. I have suggested that quality outcomes usually mean meeting all the needs involved in the complexity, not just some of them. I have suggested that achieving change requires cooperation, and that cooperation is effective in confronting inappropriate bureaucratic inflexibilities. Cooperation, negotiation and confronting complexity rather than denying it will almost certainly involve acting in multiprofessional concert rather than bureaucratic isolation. Bureaucratic organisation works for the simple; anti-bureaucratic social work is needed for the complex and the complex is nearly always multiprofessional. So if anti-bureaucratic social work is to be successful, it must work multiprofessionally.

Anti-bureaucratic practice and anti-oppressive practice

Anti-bureaucratic social work involves respect for people and for organisations, not for one or the other. So far I have been discussing what I have called anti-bureaucratic social work as though it was something new and different. As we approach the end of this Chapter, it will be evident that it fits with good practice in all sorts of different ways. It also has a ring about it: in an ironic way I have tried to draw attention to my argument by using a form of words which is familiar in another context: anti-discriminatory social work, anti-oppressive social work, both terms that have become familiar in the 1990s.

Anti-bureaucratic social work is closely related to anti-oppressive and anti-discriminatory practice. Good anti-bureaucratic practice will contribute to anti-oppressive and anti-discriminatory practice because bureaucratic behaviour often has oppressive and discriminatory effects. Using formal or legal language discriminates against people from an ethnic minority group whose English is not very good, or who do not understand the local government system very well. They will lose even more than someone who is more at ease with English and has grown up in the system.

Taking this further, anti-discriminatory and anti-oppressive practice needs to incorporate a concern for anti-bureaucratic practice. This is because bureaucratic behaviour can sometimes offer a way of concealing discrimination and oppression behind a veil of legal and proper behaviour.

I have also suggested that bureaucratic behaviour is a way of sustaining our own feeling of power and our own control of the situation. We use the formulas to avoid the complexity and pressure involved in being truly open and to feel better about the fact that the situation is confusing and stressful for us too. So, bureaucratic behaviour is often a sign that behind it is someone or some group trying to hang on to their own power in the situation. Anti-oppressive and anti-discriminatory practice tries to combat just that hanging onto power. Bureaucratic behaviour, then, offers a clue to the fact that oppressive and discriminatory behaviour might be going on.

After these pointers to the nature of social work practice which is anti-bureaucratic, I want to turn in the next Chapter to the broader implications of the argument. If social workers must tackle some of the ill-effects of bureaucracy and managerialism, what does this mean for social work as an activity and a profession, and for the organisations?

Chapter 5
SOCIAL WORK'S ANTI-BUREAUCRATIC ROLE

Bureaucracy, managerialism and change – the problems

We started from social workers' experiences of social work being constrained by over-bureaucratic behaviour. It is a problem in the perception of social workers, and also for their clients and the managements of the social services. It is a worsening problem and we have examined the reasons why. Social changes have led to a more diverse society, which expects greater flexibility within its services. On the other hand, political changes have imposed managerialism on the public services in which most social work is done. Managerialism imposes a controlling ethos which runs against the flexibility which social changes increasingly demand.

We are having to respond to a diverse and rapidly changing society. The diversity is more than individuals can integrate in their minds. The change is faster than some people want and not fast enough for others. The settlement about the way we organise society is breaking down. Therefore, we have to establish a way of life which accepts and lives with diversity and change. Social work has to contribute to that. Aiming for anti-oppressive, empowering practice is one way in which we struggle for good practice that helps people cope with the way they must live and change. We cannot have diversity if people are oppressed by social divisions which exclude certain parts of the diversity. At the moment, some groups are excluded from influence, from consideration and from pursuing their own interests and needs.

But resources create or limit capacity to change: personal, emotional, physical, health, and financial resources. The more you have the easier it is to change; the more you have the easier it is to cocoon yourself away from unpleasantnesses that you do not want to know about. The people social workers deal with have often lost their resources to manage change. Sometimes they never had the resources in the first place. They are excluded from obtaining the resources they need. Our services and society have to become more flexible and more accepting of diversity in order to offer excluded groups the resources they need to participate fully in society.

In Chapter 3, I presented the arguments for advocacy both as a professional role and also as a service development strategy. I suggested, looking at it broadly, that it would strengthen the capacity and opportunities for excluded groups to participate in society. At least, focusing on our direct professional concerns, it would improve their impact in the social services or services where we can help them participate and gain influence. In Chapter 4, I argued that

81

social workers should try to help their clients overcome bureaucratic inflexibility wherever it gets in the way of the right help for clients.

Advocacy and anti-bureaucratic practice involve not only working with clients but also engaging with organisations, both our own and others. Taking this further, I want to suggest that the 21st century will need a new professional strategy about the relationship between social work and the organisations in which it operates. We must recast it so that we can accept and play out our anti-bureaucratic role effectively. This would benefit both our clients and the organisations and societies that we serve. It helps all three because it is a personal help strategy, but it also speaks to the social and organisational changes that we have been examining. We need to organise social work and the social services to achieve a different, more flexible and pluralistic approach to management and policy-making. To make it work, we need to reinforce that approach with education and training. An important aspect of the new settlement for the role of social work in society is an anti-bureaucratic role and a new form of social work.

Obviously, if we are going to do this in social services, we should perhaps be considering similar moves in other public services. I believe modern conditions and the wishes and needs of citizens in the 21st century will increasingly require it. This would enable social work to fit more easily into the public services. However, the point of this book is the special role and responsibility of social work as anti-bureaucratic. Therefore, I argue that social work must move now and not wait to change the whole public sector.

Still, before considering these requirements for social work's anti-bureaucratic role, we must first question whether this is a legitimate concern for social work. Two issues are: is taking up an anti-bureaucratic role appropriate at all and should social work be the profession that focuses on being anti-bureaucratic?

Changing government – plural structures
Chapter 1 noted the arguments for bureaucracy. Well-implemented, it may help to create stability, neutrality and certainty of responsibility and accountability in an organisation. It permits clarity of management, or at least of administration. We also saw that bureaucracy is not necessarily bad. The problem is inflexible behaviour which seems to grow up in bureaucratic organisations. And I argued that much of Britain's inflexible bureaucratic behaviour comes from its centralised and legalistic system of government. A more open and pluralistic system would help us to be less inflexibly bureaucratic.

In the latter part of the 1990s, Britain's system of government is beginning to change. Already, there are assemblies in Wales, Scotland and eventually Northern Ireland. There are regional organisations in the English regions and it is possible that stronger regional government will emerge, as in much of the rest of Europe. Experiments with different forms of management are going on in local government. There are proposals to change the voting system which may, if they are implemented, lead to a more pluralist political system. The reform of the House of Lords is likely to create a political structure which has more political legitimacy than the present House. This will provide another pluralist element in the British system. European Union political structures are also becoming more important. It is hard to see where all this might lead, but the consequence may be, as the 21st century progresses, a greater acceptance of pluralism in British political life.

Dunleavy and O'Leary (1987) distinguish two forms of pluralism. One suggests that the power of government is constrained by its many relationships and interactions with other institutions in 'civil society'. Neo-pluralism points to the increasing influence of business in these interactions, because of the importance of the economy. Representative institutions and class interests become less important where economic and business interests are crucial to decision-making. So, external control of government by 'checks and balances' among different social and political institutions is less effective in those areas of business. However, where a particular area of policy-making does not affect business, other networks of policy interests and influence are still important. Political institutions become less important as economic management is given overarching priority. Professionalised bureaucracies gain more influence in the policy-making process because of this, if they do not interfere with business and economic interests. We might surmise, then, that business and economic interests will leave policy-making in the social services to those interested. However, this will only hapen if business and economic interests are not engaged in social services issues. We can achieve this by keeping social services costs out of political controversy.

However, the conventional trade-off in neo-pluralism between bureaucracy and the professions may not be maintained. The bureau-professional 'settlement' that we reviewed in Chapter 2 suggests that professional discretion tempers the inflexibility of bureaucratic systems. However, I have also suggested that social work and the social services cannot go down that route. This is because the demands to deal flexibly with diversity and change prevent the imposition of new professional constraints on flexible responses to plural political authorities, consumerism and advocacy. Mintzberg's (1979) analysis of the possibilities for more flexibly structured organisations (see Chapter 2) suggests that we must look for more flexible relations between social work and its organisational environment.

Social services in plural structures

What will be the role of social work and the social services in these changed circumstances? First, the state will not have one centralised power. Of course, in complex societies it never has had, but it will be clearer that a range of policies, practices and sources of authority have the right of acceptance. There will be more alternative and more complex systems of accountability. Community, local, regional, national and European forms of government will have different kinds of impact on different aspects of society. Their authority will develop from many different kinds of influence.

Secondly, however, we should not assume the priority of any one structure for accountability. The European Union, for example, has a largely economic policy remit. It implements social policy to the extent that it promotes an economic 'level playing field' among different regions of Europe. The Scottish Parliament and the Northern Ireland and Welsh Assemblies will probably have more influence on local social services policy than UK policy-making. There will be economic bodies in the English regions. If devolution to the nations of the British Isles is successful, stronger regional government in England will follow based on these bodies. Social services powers are a likely candidate for devolution here too. At an even lower level and more informally, local, community and informal networks are developing as part of commissioning. Different forms of participation and action arise as government withdraws from substantial community roles. These changes will also offer an important constituency for making demands and giving authority to action and decisions of social services and social workers.

Opportunities for influence from a variety of groups will grow from these changes. Stronger professionalisation, so that social work can take its place as one of the influential professions in the bureaucracy is not the way forward. This is because wider interests will contest any power-play of this kind. In the new political world, a range of influences is relevant. Among them are service users (the people who are customers for services), clients (the people whom social workers help in a developmental way), carers, and many citizens and communities around people who use the social services. Beyond that, colleagues in related professions have a concern for cooperation with the social services. This means that they have an interest in how social workers do their jobs and organise their services. Unless we are prepared to change and respond to other professionals, we cannot have multiprofessional services, which provide a 'seamless' service. Also, we could not collaborate to prevent danger and difficulty for members of the public. We have noted that public safety and a response to public concerns is a requirement equally of the social services as it is of all public services. We cannot just focus on service users and clients.

Citizen-responsive, user-involved multiprofessional social work
The future for social work, then, is:

- *citizen-responsive*, concerned to respond to citizens with an interest in the public role of social work;

- *user-involved*, where social work collaborates with clients, service users and the user community, and

- *multiprofessional*, collaborating with related colleagues.

However, social work should still be managed and respond to corporate political policies. We must develop forms of regulation, planning and practice which respond to the interests of all these groups. We cannot put one above the other. Users and clients are citizens, but not all citizens are users and clients. Non-user citizens have and press interests in the social services. Concerning ourselves only with individual ethics in relationships with clients is an avoidance of our responsibilities to non-user citizens. We cannot put clients' needs above public safety; we cannot put professional cooperation above the wishes of service users; we cannot put responding to public anxieties above the needs of socially excluded service users and clients.

Fortunately, present proposals for the regulation of social work suggest that movement towards this pattern is already taking place. It will create a new and more appropriate balance between the user, the professional and the organisation. The proposals in the White Paper for England (DoH, 1998), are likely to be echoed, with differences, in the other UK countries. They suggest regional regulators (Care Commissions) building on the pre-existing Social Services Inspectorate and arm's-length inspection units for residential care and other facilities. A General Social Care Council will regulate social care employees. Its membership will contain a majority of non-social workers, particularly fellow professionals and service user representatives. This is surely a concrete organisational sign of the trends discussed above. The purpose of this Council is not to establish social work as a 'genuine' profession. Instead, it aims to protect the public and develop the profession's capacity to serve.

With other professions, similar developments are taking place. The government is, at the time of writing, criticising the Law Society's mechanisms for dealing with complaints, and threatening that a statutory body could take over. After various scandals, the medical colleges have been required to manage clinical effectiveness more directly. Various mechanisms such as NICE, the National Institute for Clinical Effectiveness, have been established. In higher education, an institute for teaching and learning to strengthen teaching quality, a Quality Assurance Agency and regular reviews of teaching and research have been established. In teaching, a stronger inspectorial regime, control of aims and quality through the Qualifications and Curriculum Authority (but associated with a General Teaching Council) is to be established.

The pattern is similar: greater formal regulation on behalf of the public, with a diminution of control by the profession itself, built on a more flexible and market-oriented organisational structure inherited and developed from the previous Conservative administration. This forms the basis for a more user-oriented approach. However, this model does not permit more flexibility if the answer to political control is bureaucracy. It can only be effective if the added structure of professional regulation permits greater discretion to the professionals. However, this discretion is more strongly regulated in itself rather than through the bureaucracy. The final element in many of these examples is better-quality practice, enforced through regular inspection but built up through more effective training. This is also an element of the social services package of changes. The new national training organisations in each country will develop structures for training. Inevitably, the General Social Care Councils and Care Commissions will press for professional training and post-experience, continuing professional development for improving standards.

What will social work practice be like if these organisational and social developments take place? Citizen-responsive, user-involved multiprofessional social work will look outwards with a concern for the needs that citizens in the community have for social work. It will involve users in not only working towards their own needs and wishes, but recognising and taking on citizens' and the community's wishes for the shape of their social environment. And it will use multiprofessional assessments – no one profession can apply all the skills and knowledge that clients and citizens need. Citizens and users will not be satisfied with a partial service or one which fails to respond to all aspects of citizen, community and user needs and wishes.

The new social work services must be anti-bureaucratic
That social work will be anti-bureaucratic. It will have three aims:

- It will respond to a wide range of social and citizen needs and will reject the bureaucratic secrecy and lack of concern for broad social needs. It must do so because the new consumerised market-experienced citizen and the new empowered community will accept nothing less.

- It will involve the user, because it is more effective and doing so reflects professional values. User involvement is important because the diversity of people and social aspirations we will work with will require assessment of the individual's needs and wishes. Generalised assumptions about what is required do not meet the needs of diverse populations.

- It will involve other professionals, because there is an increasing range of professionals with well-developed valuable skills to offer. Doing the best for citizens and user will require pulling in all of them.

However, those three directions for future practice are sometimes in conflict. The implication of anti-bureaucratic social work, therefore, is that these three directions of development should be held in balance openly, not secretly. The fear is that we hold the balance oppressively. For example, a mentally ill offender who might be dangerous to others could be intimidated by constantly being reminded what a risk he is to other people. Therefore, we cannot only respond to citizens' demands for public protection to have absolute priority – risks must be taken. In another example, local people's feelings might be ignored when they complain about the disorganisation and noise caused by clients who are unsatisfactory neighbours and tenants. Therefore, we must concern ourselves with the freedoms and rights of all citizens, not just with those of our clients. In yet another example, a professional colleague's work might be damaged if information they received in a clinical setting is used without permission to take child protection proceedings. Therefore, we cannot place clients or the public at risk while pursuing the professional cooperation that a bureaucracy might demand. I have used these three examples to show that we cannot just operate as social workers with a single view of what we should do: the interaction between the responses of users, the community and professional colleagues will have to be constantly considered. I tried to show in Chapter 4 that a focus on 'the client' is not enough. Our concern must be for the client's needs within the pattern of community life and the network of services (see Figure 4.1).

We must not ignore or be immobilised by these daily conflicts of interest. Instead, we must openly embrace them and gain the consent of citizens in the community, clients and users and professional colleagues. We should create a balance between the constituencies and interests which works for them all.

Social work practice should be anti-bureaucratic

It is integral to what social workers do on behalf of users, community and professional colleagues, therefore, that they act anti-bureaucratically. The task is dealing with the interaction of the individual's needs, the community's wishes and the roles of other professionals and their agencies. Therefore, social workers' roles involve sorting out the inflexibilities in the connections between these three factors. They do this on behalf of other services just as they do on behalf of service users. They do it because citizens in the community expect services to operate cooperatively. This is because complex and difficult life experiences need interpreting for other services which are set up to deal with people more formulaically. Social work is there to help other organisations deal with the complexities and the exceptions.

Does this mean, then, that the anti-bureaucratic role is always going to be there? Can we never sigh with relief that other organisations are going to deal with people flexibly and positively? The answer is: to some extent. Some of the time, as we saw in Chapters 3 and 4 anti-bureaucratic practice engages with and tries to change organisational systems: our own and those of other organisations. Obviously, therefore we might hope for improvements. Citizens will demand them. Also, we can hope that other colleagues in other professions and organisations are just as concerned about inflexibility and bureaucratic behaviour as we are. So they will always be seeking improvements, too.

However, bureaucratic control is integral to most organisations, especially where inexperienced or untrained staff are used in large numbers to process human lives. Computers will improve this, and are becoming ever more flexible. Nonetheless, anyone who has used one will know that a computer thinks in the way the (usually American) programmer thinks. You are always obliged to fit in with that way of thinking. Inevitably, therefore, we will always need anti-bureaucratic social work to act for people who have to be fitted into less than human systems.

If social workers claim to change bureaucratic practice in their own and other agencies, they have to display good non-bureaucratic practice to others. Social workers will not get people coming to them for help in dealing with bureaucracy elsewhere, if they present themselves as bureaucrats. People will just not understand that social workers can help them with bureaucracy elsewhere if they think social work itself is mired in bureaucracy.

Related to that, social workers need to be successful in using interpersonal skills with service users. You cannot do this behind stacks of forms within which the users' complex world has been categorised in tick-boxes. It is just as impossible behind the lap top with its structured information system although some members of the public are more comfortable with the impersonality of a computer enquiry. Social work sets out to personalise, individualise and humanise the social services. It is a particular and valuable role which bureaucrats cannot perform very well.

Another point is that non-bureaucratic service is generally better, more accept-able service; more acceptable to users, to citizens in the community and to professional colleagues. It is more flexible and more responsive to a service user's individuality. Bureaucratic behaviour divides whole people up into col-lections of social categories, just as bad medical practice divides whole people up into collections of symptoms and diagnoses. We complain, quite rightly, about treating patients as though they are a walking diagnosis. We should complain just as strongly about treating people as a 'child protection case' or a 'community care assessment'.

So social work has to be anti-bureaucratic within its own agencies. This will always produce a problem for social workers, because to some extent they always have to be in opposition to their agencies. Some people might also suggest that this is unrealistic because how can you be against your employers? Do they not have the ultimate power?

We have seen in previous chapters that the answer is: 'yes, but that power is tempered by several factors'. First, social work agencies are public bodies or are governed by altruistic purposes contained in their constitution. Secondly, anyone who works in an organisation, and especially people at the top of the organisation, knows that there are always competing and conflicting activities and purposes. Thirdly, there is no point in employing someone to do the detailed work with service users and then ignoring what they say is needed. So advocating within an agency on behalf of service users is a skill in using factors which are on the side of users against the factors that are against them. Social workers need to develop that skill. The fact that it is a recognised aspect of their job supports them in doing so. Another support is the increasing recognition of advocacy services as part of the social services system.

Social services should be managed anti-bureaucratically

If social services are anti-bureaucratic in their aims and social workers are working anti-bureaucratically, it follows that they need to be managed anti-bureaucratically. Managers must manage in ways which respect the importance of advocacy and anti-bureaucratic practice. Because advocacy and anti-bureau-cratic practice require engagement with changing the organisation, our own and others that we work with, it will be engaging with management.

If we accept advocacy and anti-bureaucratic roles, social work organisations must change to accommodate this role within themselves. Agencies have to be more accepting of their workers' representing the needs and views of service users. My experience, described in Chapter 3, where agencies use bureaucratic inflexibilities to ration, is an unacceptable approach to the social responsibility of the social services.

Are bureaucratic attitudes just out-of-date and incompetent management, which will disappear as management skills and training develop in the public services in general and social services in particular? Mullender and Perrott (1998) argue that management is becoming feminised, less 'macho', less controlling. New techniques focus on teamwork and co-operation rather than individualism and domination. A range of possible ways of managing are available, but there always have been different managers make different choices. Trends may arise in one direction or the other. Now, they are towards this openness and flexibility. Nevertheless, bureaucracy and managerialism will always be available to be reasserted by ideologies which need them, or by organisations which do not actively avoid them.

Because anti-bureaucratic practice is a crucial role of social work, the organisation of the profession needs to reflect that. Similarly, the state and the political system of authority needs to give discretionary powers in an organised way: not to pass on responsibility and blame but to manage an authority system which recognises flexibility and discretion. We have seen, in the early part of this Chapter, that movements are taking place which will make this more possible. Alternative, flexible structures which involve stronger teamwork and rely less on structured controls are possible and, in some areas of organisation, desirable. I have argued in this book that this is vitally necessary for social work. This is because social work's anti-bureaucratic role means that flexibility in a complex set of issues and relationships is essential. We cannot carry on with the restrictions of a bureaucratic system any longer. However, we do not need to exchange these for another set of professional restrictions. We need to withdraw from managerialism, because this is imposing inconsistent and inappropriate ways of working on the social services. A new form of management and accountability for service is being created.

The requirement of agencies, therefore, is to be more explicit about the requirements for flexibility. We need a new settlement of the question of discretion. The boundaries and operation of discretion need to be established and enforced. Just as social workers need to accept and use discretion, so politicians and the state need to define and encourage appropriate discretion. Agencies must withdraw from managerialism, because it is strangling what we need the social services for.

Anti-bureaucratic social work means changes in education and training
Developing anti-bureaucratic practice and advocacy has implications for education and training. Much social work education focuses on interpersonal therapeutic skills, or the skills of group and community change, but does not focus on working within and changing organisations. The skills of advocacy, negotiating

and planning for users' needs to be met within agencies are still underdeveloped. Moreover, managerialism has infected education. A 'performance culture' in agencies leads to demands that education and training be focused on meeting agencies' objectives. Education and training have other valid responsibilites such as developing refelcetive practice, which must place agency objectives in context. Education is not there soley to enable agencies to pursue their aims, but also to promote the personal development of staff. Therefore the new settlement needs to identify and manage an education system which puts agency perfomance alongside personal development as equally valid aims.

However, developing anti-bureaucratic social work requires more than that. Good education and training is vital to making new management, new accountability and new anti-bureaucratic practice roles effective. We saw above that education at all levels is essential for the new settlement between the economic and political system and the bureau-professional system to work itself out. Social workers need to be educated to accept and use discretion. Anti-bureaucratic education means understanding more complex ways of developing and responding to accountabilities to citizens, communities, users and to professional colleagues. The whole standard and level of social work education needs to be enhanced, and its value needs to be recognised and accepted by managements of agencies. Part of withdrawing from managerialism is the acceptance that much higher and more complex levels of capacity must be provided through training. At the moment, most of the social services offer minimal advanced training. People are worried that basic skill training is not there; they are worried about the inadequacy of the basic professional qualification. Rightly so, but that does not exclude the need for continuing education in more advanced skills. The new post-qualification training in child protection needs to be the first step in a much broader range of training. As with child protection, such training will protect clients and users, and improve the capacity to use professional skills. It will protect organisations by enhancing professional capacity. Improved education will also strengthen the confidence of other professions and services in social work.

Better education and training giving a greater capacity to be critical of what you are doing is an essential part of being anti-bureaucratic. Inevitably, that means being more critical of what is going on in an agency and about the practical consequences of political decisions. However, we need to be just as critical of our own role and our own, sometimes undesirable, impact on clients and the social services system. This means social workers having a greater degree of individual practitioner responsibility which, as we saw in Chapter 2, is one of the assumptions about professional responsibility. However, we are not looking here for traditional forms of individual practitioner accountability but for new forms of accountability in a more complex and diverse society.

This will require a different organisational context for social services. We saw in Chapter 4 that being anti-bureaucratic means being more open with clients and users, encouraging them to use their rights to complain and seek reviews of our decisions. Defensive management is out of place in this kind of situation. 'Why are we always getting these appeals against your department?' the Chief Executive asks the Director of Social Services. 'Why is it whenever one of your social workers gets hold of a tenant, we get all kinds of legalistic demands?' the Director of Housing asks the same Director. The answer very often is not: 'This is their right that we're helping them to take up.' Very often the good depart-ment is the quiet department, and the managers of staff who encourage clients (these members of the public with their rights) to complain or press their views will be criticised for not staying in control. Yet in the consumer-empowered world of the 21st century, defensiveness looks discreditable. We need to be able to stand on our evident skills and knowledge and develop a capacity to explain what we are doing in ways that people will understand.

The answer to this is to be right, to be generous and to be fair, and to help people understand why and how they have been treated correctly, generously and fairly. Partly, this is about openness again. We miss out explaining what was done and why, so citizens cannot understand how reasonable we have been. We do not or cannot take the time to put the decision in context, so clients cannot understand the appropriateness of our decision in the circumstances.

Too much discretion = too much power over users?
Do we want social workers to have the kind of professional autonomy which wide discretion implies? It might mean that service users lose 'rights' in favour of social workers' discretion? Might this lead social workers to have more power when they are trying to empower their clients? Would too much discre-tion disempower clients?

There are three answers to the 'professional autonomy' issue. The first is: no, only if we let it. The second is: yes, you have to have power and discretion yourself before you can use it to empower, and by using your own power alongside service users you add to their potential power. Related to this is the third point: using power in any social situation does not necessarily take power away from someone else. It may mean that more power is being used overall.

Anti-bureaucracy: a fuss over nothing?
Finally, is all this a fuss over nothing? Has the management world of social work and of local authorities changed? Governments in the 1990s have emphasised part-nership, responsiveness to service users, participation and effective involvement of

advocacy to give voices to citizens and service users. A major effort has gone into developing better quality services. So is all this fuss over managerialism and bureaucracy really harking back to problems in the past which good agencies have overcome.

Bureaucratic and inflexible behaviour is never finally overcome; it is always a tendency in a large organisation. When change is in the air, when everything is in flux, when there is strong commitment to flexibility, participation and partnership, then inflexibility begins to recede. But as certainty returns, as conventions are re-established, as complaints and appeals are heard, the openness begins to be replaced by conventions and rules. And rightly so: because people need to understand where they are, there has to be equity and clarity along with the flexibility. Still, when we make the shift towards greater equity and certainty, it becomes more likely that we will also be shifting towards inflexibility and bureaucracy.

So we always need to be alert for excessive inflexibility, excessive compliance with the rules, excessive demands of managerialism, acquiescence to the needs of the agency, cynicism about the needs of service users. These failings will always flow back into a service like water will always seep back into a container with a hole.

Is it right that any public service, perhaps any service, is formed mainly by the needs of management? Of course we would want a service to be as efficient as possible. But efficient to what end? The implication of managerialism and bureaucracy is that the end is imposed from above, in pursuit of particular policies and strategic political objectives. No profession and no activity, even wholly commercial business, is immune from the planning and purposes of those in political power. It is right that, in a democratic society, the taxpayer who elects a government is entitled to a say in what services are provided. We accept in paying taxes which support railways and buses that we may not use them ourselves, but we expect them to be worthwhile and responsive to the needs of others. So, meeting the political objectives set on behalf of taxpayers and society generally is at least partly balanced by services being responsive to the wishes of those who use them.

The point goes further with professional services. The purpose of employing people with particular expertise is that, to a certain extent, they should have free rein in deciding what should be done. Since we are calling on their expertise, then we would not want to second-guess it, given some reasonable safeguards. So social work and social services require a balance to be struck between the three elements. The social services must balance the managerial implementation of political policy, the wishes and requirements of service users and the expertise of the professionals who provide the service. Each worker must also achieve a balance, because the political system and the agency only partly represents the stakeholders involved. Workers must balance the needs of citizens in the community with clients' needs and the needs of professional colleagues. The argument of this book is, in essence, that the balance is wrong at the moment and has been for quite a while. Managerialism implemented through excessively bureaucratic behaviour has too much influence. It is time for social work to accept the value of strong knowledge-based practice and a degree of independence from managerial and state control as a fundamental requirement of effectiveness.

We need to go further and look at the way professional expertise can defend service users against the state. In the late 1980s, for example, social workers struggled to achieve a less discriminatory and oppressive service and more anti-discriminatory and anti-oppressive practice. They did so against the vituperation of press and a conservative establishment. However, discrimination and racism are apparent in other public services, so we should be grateful that social work tried to achieve a better approach. Some socialist writers assume that the democratic freedoms within the state are the major defences against oppression. However, many marginalised and excluded people find the state just as oppressive as any social or class division. People who lived through the governments of the 1980s and '90s found the state no protection against the oppression and social exclusion.

Pluralism offers the opportunity for alternative sources of support and defence to be made available. Community organisations, trade unions, family and friends: many mechanisms for support and co-operation might be avenues of protection. Professionals doing their job following the requirements of professional and ethical conduct provide just such an alternative source of thinking and organisation. We need the value, knowledge and skill base of professionals such as social workers. This is not to claim that they are the only defence, or that they have a monopoly of concern and action. Of course not, and there have been times when they have been allied with oppression. As an extreme example, Lorenz (1994) describes the complicity of social workers in the Nazi period in Germany in one of the worst periods of the 20th century. However, having available alternative organisational and knowledge structures is a crucial part of the defence of democracy. Their flexibility and independence from bureaucratic control is integral to playing a part in that plural universe.

So as we look towards the 21st century, we can hope that it will be a better period than the 20th. We all have to make a contribution to that. Every contribution will be small but it will be part of a whole. The social work contribution will not be arrogant independent practice, but user-involved, citizen-responsive multiprofessional practice. This anti-bureaucratic practice accepts and carries out its accountability to these three constituencies as well as to the political and organisational structures in which it works. If it acts like this, overcoming some of the weaknesses of its management and organisation in recent decades will offer the basis for a stronger growth in the future.

BIBLIOGRAPHY

Ad Hoc Committee on Advocacy (1969) 'The social worker as advocate: champions of social victims' *Social Work* 14(2), pp16–21

Attlee, C R (1920) *The Social Worker* London, Bell

Barclay Report (1982) *Social Workers: their role and tasks* London, Bedford Square Press

BASW (1996) *A Code of Ethics for Social Work* Birmingham, BASW

Bateman, N (1995) *Advocacy Skills: a handbook for human service professionals* Aldershot, Hants, Gower

Brandon, D, Brandon, A and Brandon, T (1995) *Advocacy: power to people with disabilities* Birmingham, Venture

Burns, T and Stalker, G M (1966) *The Management of Innovation* (2nd edn.) London, Tavistock

Children Act, 1989

Clarke, J and Newman, J (1997) *The Managerial State: power, politics and ideology in the remaking of social welfare* London, Sage

Dalrymple, J and Hough, J (eds) (1995) *Having a Voice: an exploration of children's rights and advocacy* Birmingham, Venture

Dalrymple, J and Payne, M (eds). (1995) *'They listened to him': Report to the Gulbenkian Foundation* Manchester: ASC and Department of Applied Community Studies, The Manchester Metropolitan University

DoH (1998) *Modernising Social Services* London, HMSO

DoH (1999) *A New Approach to Social Services Performance: consultation document*, London, Department of Health

Dunleavy, P and O'Leary, B (1987) *Theories of the State: the politics of liberal democracy* London, Macmillan

Emerson, D, Taylor, R and Payne, M (1994) *Report of the Warrington Mental Health Advocacy Project* Manchester, Department of Applied Community Studies, The Manchester Metropolitan University

Gerth, H H and Mills, C W (eds). (1948) *From Max Weber: essays in sociology* London, Routledge and Kegan Paul

Hadley, R and Clough, R (1996) *Care in Chaos: frustration and challenge in community care* London, Cassell

Hague, R, Harrop, M and Breslin, S (1998) *Comparative Government and Politics: an introduction* London, Macmillan

Hall, P (1976) *Reforming the Welfare* London, Heinemann

Hunt, G and Campbell, D (1998) 'Social workers speak out' in Hunt, G. (ed.) *Whistleblowing in the Social Services: public accountability and professional practice*. London, Arnold, pp147–64

Ife, J (1997) *Rethinking Social Work: towards critical practice*, Melbourne, Longman

Jacques, E (1990) 'In praise of hierarchy', *Harvard Business Review* (Jan-Feb, 1990), pp127–33

Levy, A and Kahan, B (1991) *The Pindown Experience and the Protection of Children: Report of the Staffordshire Child Care Inquiry*, 1990 Stafford, Staffordshire County Council

Lewis, J and Glennester, H (1996) *Implementing the New Community Care* Buckingham, Open University Press

Lorenz, W (1994) *Social Work in a Changing Europe* London, Routledge

Middleton, L (1994) 'The tyranny of procedure' *Professional Social Work*, December, p6.

Mintzberg, H (1979) *The Structuring of Organisations: a synthesis of the research* Englewood Cliffs, NJ, Prentice-Hall

Morgan, G (1997) *Images of Organisation* (Rev. edn.) Thousand Oaks, CA, Sage

Mullender, A and Perrott, S (1998) 'Social work and organisations' in Adams, R, Dominelli, L and Payne, M (eds). *Social Work: themes, issues and critical debates*, London, Macmillan, pp67–77

National Health Service and Community Care Act, 1990

Payne, M (1982) *Working in Teams* London, Macmillan

Payne, M (1995) *Social Work and Community Care* London, Macmillan

Pfeffer, N and Coote, A (1991) *Is Quality Good for You? A critical review of quality assurance in welfare services* London, Institute for Public Policy Research

Pollitt, C (1993) *Managerialism and the Public Services: cuts or cultural change in the 1990s?* Oxford, Blackwell

Potter, J (1988) 'Consumerism and the public sector: how well does the coat fit?' *Public Administration* 66(2), pp149–64

Powell, R. (1998) 'Managerial procedure and professional practice in social work' in Hunt, G. (ed.) *Whistleblowing in the Social Services: public account-ability and professional practice.* London, Arnold, 165-84.

Rees, S (1991) *Achieving Power: practice and policy in social welfare* N. Sydney, Allen and Unwin

Seebohm Report (1968) *Report of the Committee on Local Authority and Allied Personal Social Services* (Cmnd 3703), London, HMSO

Silverman, D (1970) *The Theory of Organisations: a sociological framework* London, Heinemann

UKCC (1984) *Exercising Accountability: a framework to assist nurses, midwives and health visitors to consider ethical aspects of professional practice* London, United Kingdom Central Council for Nursing, Midwifery and Health Visiting

Wagner Report (1988) *A Positive Choice* London, HMSO

Weale, A (1978) *Equality and Social Policy* London, Routledge and Kegan Paul

Williams, F (1992) 'Somewhere over the rainbow: universality and diversity in social policy' in Manning, N and Page, R (eds). *Social Policy Review 4* Canterbury, Social Policy Asssociation, pp?

Wootton, B (1959) *Social Science and Social Pathology* London, Allen and Unwin

INDEX

accountability 4, 5, 6, 8, 11-14, 24, 45, 61, 84, 90-1

    see also: individual practitioner accountability, responsibility

Ad Hoc Committee on Advocacy 46

adhocracy 11

advocacy 40, 41-57, 61, 72, 81-2, 89

    as an aspect of social work 41, 45-7, 54

        as a service for users 41, 54

        case 43, 46, 52

        cause 43, 46, 67

        citizen 43

        group 43-4

        peer 44

        professional 44

        self- 43-4

agency 47, 49-55, 61, 64, 68-70, 89, 91

altruism 89

anti-bureaucratic practice 2, 5, 6, 33, 40, 41, 42, 59-80, 81-2, 89, 91-4

    definition 61

anti-oppressive practice 79-81, 94

assessment 12, 33, 63

Attlee, C. R. 45

Audit Commission 17

authority 6-8, 10, 13, 14, 41, 45, 70, 76, 79, 84

autonomy 25, 92

best interests 33, 54

Barclay Report 38

Bateman, N. 46

blame 11, 13, 19, 90

Brandon, A, D. and T. 43

Breslin, S. 14

British Association of Social Workers (BASW) 23, 45

Bronze standard practice 64-7

bureaucracy iii, 2-22, 63-5, 68, 70-2, 74, 79-80, 83, 86, 88, 93

bureaucratic behaviour 2, 4, 5, 14, 20, 59, 62, 75-7, 80, 81, 8994

    definition 2

bureau-professionals 10, 36, 38, 83

Burns, T. 10

Campbell, D. 34

care management 28

Case Conference 23

centralisation 14, 18, 29, 37, 82, 84

certainty 7, 26

charismatic authority 6-7

child protection 32, 35, 48, 72-4, 89

Children Act 1989 38, 51

choice 32-3

citizen, -ship 3, 25-6, 39, 43, 84-7, 89, 9194

    - advocacy see advocacy

civil society 20, 83

clarity 7, 26, 57, 75-7

Clarke, J 25, 38

class 19-20, 83

clienthood, clients iii, 5-6, 34, 37, 41, 44-5, 48-50, 64

    see also: service users

clinical responsibility 24

    see also: accountability, responsibility

Clough, R. 34

cognitive-behavioural theory 40

community care 21, 28, 32, 33, 34, 35, 47, 57, 89

community physicians 23

community work 49

    see also: youth and community work